METROPOLITAN INCOME GROWTH AND CONVERGENCE

T0347471

Metropolitan Income Growth and Convergence

ROBERTO J. CAVAZOS
The University of Texas at San Antonio

Routledge
Taylor & Francis Group

LONDON AND NEW YORK

First published 2001 by Ashgate Publishing

Reissued 2018 by Routledge
2 Park Square, Milton Park, Abingdon, Oxon OX14 4RN
711 Third Avenue, New York, NY 10017, USA

Routledge is an imprint of the Taylor & Francis Group, an informa business

Publisher's Note
The publisher has gone to great lengths to ensure the quality of this reprint but points out that some imperfections in the original copies may be apparent.

Disclaimer
The publisher has made every effort to trace copyright holders and welcomes correspondence from those they have been unable to contact.

A Library of Congress record exists under LC control number: 2001090179

ISBN 13: 978-1-138-73041-0 (hbk)
ISBN 13: 978-1-138-73032-8 (pbk)
ISBN 13: 978-1-315-18945-1 (ebk)

Contents

List of Tables

Acknowledgements

I thank all those who assisted me in this undertaking. In particular, Professor Brian J.L. Berry who has never ceased providing me with encouragement, guidance and sage advice. Similarly, Professors James C. Murdoch and Barry Seldon of The University of Texas at Dallas, have been key to this effort and to my academic career. Without their help and generous support, this work would not be complete.

Certainly, my family and many friends gave the encouragement and support to enable me to complete this study. All have contributed, and their support continues to aid me in all my professional efforts.

1 Introduction

Why do some cities grow and others wither? Ever since the founding of the Republic there has always been some scheme or another afoot to attract individuals and business enterprises to a particular site. Since the early colonies to the eager embellishment of late 19th century "boosterism" and the creation of chambers of commerce, Americans have been quite determined to ensure continued growth for their cities. The question is what determines urban growth? Much has been written on particular causes and incidents which can explain the rise of one metropolis and the fall of another. Yet, these can be so specific as to be anecdotal. Can general tendencies be observed? Can theories used to explain the phenomenon of economic growth for larger centers of economic activity such as nations or regions be employed to find those characteristics which encourage the growth of cities? Most importantly, what if anything can be done by public authorities to encourage or create those characteristics which encourage growth. Their inquiries have variously addressed both institutions and tendencies amongst the populace of a nation and the extent to which these contribute to future growth and, in turn, to the well being of the populace and stability of the state. Most recently, scholars examining the process of economic growth have introduced new bodies of theory and new research methods to help determine whether incomes converge or diverge during the process of growth.

Two main theoretical approaches now are utilized to examine income changes during the process of economic growth. Endogenous growth theory predicts that incomes will diverge. Neoclassical growth theory predicts conditional convergence. Endogenous growth theory ascribes to technological innovation the role of engine of economic growth, via the existence of a positive feedback mechanism that permits increasing returns to scale. Neoclassical growth theorists remain true to principles of microeconomic theory and grant capital accumulation the role of engine of economic growth; technological progress occurs outside the model and thus is "exogenous". Both theoretical approaches have found varying levels of empirical support.

Purposes of this Study

In this study the determinants of U.S. metropolitan area income growth between 1970 and 1990 are examined, and an evaluation of whether metropolitan incomes have converged or diverged is undertaken. Each of the theoretical approaches and empirical techniques utilized by contemporary researchers is deployed in a simultaneous attempt to evaluate the relative worth of proposed alternatives in the evolving body of growth theory. The strategy is to focus on three specific sets of questions that arise in the work of neoclassical growth theorists, and upon the alternatives that emerge from endogenous growth theory. I thus begin by asking:

First, whether U.S. metropolitan area economic growth as measured by growth in real per capita income can be explained via the traditional Solow-Swan neoclassical growth model, which predicts that incomes will converge over time.

Second, whether "conditional" convergence of incomes has occurred among U.S. metropolitan areas, implying that incomes have converged, but only when controlled for varying levels of different factors such as population and technology.

Third, whether conditional convergence might arise from sector-driven growth, as predicted by regional growth theory.

The alternative is that metropolitan area growth can be more satisfactorily explained using endogenous growth models. If growth is endogenous, there will be income divergence.

Fourthly, I develop and test the alternative endogenous growth models and compare their performance with the neoclassical formulations to determine which provide more insightful explanations of metropolitan growth since 1970.

In what follows, the theoretical and empirical literature is reviewed in chapters 2 and 3, the research methodology and data employed in this study are described in chapters 4 and 5. The empirical results, conclusions and possibilities for further research are presented in chapters 6 and 7.

2 Theoretical Underpinnings

In this study "growth" refers to growth in real per capita income. Growth has long been a central concern for economists and other social scientists. Without much controversy one can say that poverty has been and continues to be one of the greatest sources of human misery the world over. A direct means by which to allay poverty is through economic growth. While growth may inflict costs and other challenges it nonetheless corrects a number of problems.

Early economists, most notably Adam Smith and David Ricardo, provided much of the current framework for analyzing the process and underlying determinants of economic growth. Smith looked to the division of labor and the resulting increase in productivity as an engine of growth. He also argued for reducing trade restrictions since an open economy would permit a nation to enjoy increased rates of economic growth. Ricardo devised the notion of diminishing returns. He argued that increased investment in, say, land tended to yield less than proportionate increments to output concluding that eventually growth would cease. This could only be delayed (but not avoided) through free trade (Rostow, 1990).

The first contemporarily recognizable approach to theorizing on the determinants of economic growth was undertaken by Alfred Marshall (Robbins, 1959). Marshall, unlike his major contemporaries, focused upon growth. It is likely, according to Robbins, that Marshall acquired this particular bent as he began his career translating the work of Mill and Ricardo into the mathematical propositions utilized in modern economics. In his work Marshall sets out with a number of propositions which focus on the determinants both of income growth and its distribution. His aggregate growth model is set out below:

$$g = fI(n,e,w,F,A,S) \qquad (2.1)$$

Here g is real income of a country, n is the number and e the average efficiency of its labor force, w is amount of wealth (capital), F the fertility of its natural resources, A the state of productive arts (technology) and S the state of public security.

3

The second equation in his growth model is:

$$s = g\text{-}T\text{-}nf2(e) \tag{2.2}$$

This investment function is described as stemming from savings, s = net incomes available for saving, $f2(e)$ the average necessaries of a population whose average efficiency is e, and T taxes.
Marshall then postulates:

$$dw/dt = f3(s,D,A',i) \tag{2.3}$$

Thus the determinants of saving are broader in that they deal with issues of cultural and social variation and their effect on the savings rate, here, dw/dt is the rate of saving, D is the rate at which people discount future consumption, A' is measure of "family affections", and i is the rate of interest. To equation 3 Marshall then adds a variable E which measures the evenness of distribution of incomes, which today would be recognized as a Gini coefficient:

$$dn/dt = f4(n,e,g,E,A',D) \tag{2.4}$$
$$de/dt = f5(n,e,g,E,A',D) \tag{2.5}$$

The variable E was viewed as "measured by the ratio which the aggregate of the incomes bears to the sum of the differences between each individual income and the mean income".

Not explicit in this summary of the Marshallian system is the treatment of capital and technology. The central issue was whether the productivity of each factor of production increased or decreased with volume of work. The second focus of Marshall was to consider the effect on growth of the phenomenon of increasing returns to inputs experienced by business firms and industries.

The system laid out by Marshall was ambitious, yet to a considerable extent it presaged and underpins a number of the theoretical foundations of the approaches examined and tested in the present study. This is particularly true with respect to neoclassical growth theory. For as can be seen above, the actual determinants of productivity growth (technology) are largely determined outside the model.

Neoclassical Growth Theory

Neoclassical growth theory took its modern form in the 1950s with the work of Robert Solow and Trevor Swan (1956). Their models embody the assumption of an economy under the conditions of perfect competition. The output of this economy grows in response to larger inputs of capital and labor, and obeys the rules of diminishing returns. These assumptions result in two features of capital inputs. As the stock of capital expands, growth slows and eventually comes to a halt. For growth to continue, the economy must experience technological progress, for which the model provides no explanation: growth-inducing technological progress occurs outside of the model and is thus is exogenous. The second feature is that because poor countries (or cities) start off with less capital, they receive higher returns from initial investment, but as they grow, returns diminish. This tendency reflects the diminishing marginal productivity of capital. Ultimately, as all areas reach the same high levels of development, their growth rates will converge. The Solow-Swan growth model is expressed mathematically in a relationship illustrating the properties described above via a Cobb-Douglas type function
The Solow-Swan growth model takes the form:

$$Y = AK^a L^{1-a} \qquad\qquad (2.6)$$

here Y is output; K is capital; L is labor; $A > 0$ is the level of technology and is a constant with $0 < a < 1$. In this formulation, the assumption that the coefficients on capital and labor sum to one implies that returns to inputs follow the Cobb-Douglas specification of constant returns to scale. This can be shown by:

$$Y = f(K,L) = L \bullet F(K/L,1) = 1 \bullet f(k). \qquad\qquad (2.7)$$

In intensive form this becomes:

$$y = f(k). \qquad\qquad (2.8)$$

Here, $k = K/L$ is the capital to labor ratio, $y = Y/L$ is per capita output and the function $f(k)$ is defined to equal $F(k,1)$. The condition that can be used and in turn can be differentiated with respect to K, for fixed L, and then with respect to L for fixed K, to verify that the marginal products of the factor inputs are given:

$$\partial Y / \partial L = f'(k), \partial Y / \partial L = [f(k) - k \bullet f'(k)] \tag{2.9}$$

and

$$\partial Y / \partial L = f'(l), \partial Y / \partial K = [f(l) - l \bullet f'(l)] \tag{2.10}$$

In the model each of the inputs is essential for production, thus: $F(0,L) = F(k, 0) = f(0) = 0$. The Solow-Swan model assumes that growth stems from capital accumulation. The steady state of the capital-labor ratio can be expressed by:

$$dk / dt = s \bullet f(k) - (n + g + \delta)k, \tag{2.11}$$

where s is the saving rate, n is the rate of growth of population, g is rate of technological progress, and δ is the rate of capital depreciation, with s, n and δ exogenous.

The steady state is given by $dy / dt = 0$. This condition indicates that the approach to a steady state is a function of time. Conceptually, the steady state is defined as the case in which quantities grow at constant rates. Importantly, as the steady state is reached, an economy's output will grow at a rate equal that of population growth, and per capita growth in output reverts to 0. This can be expressed by:

$$dy / dy = df(k) / dk \bullet dk / dt = 0 \tag{2.12}$$

The consequence of this model is that the income levels of poor areas (countries, states, cities) and those of rich ones converge. When economies with lower capital per person grow more rapidly than richer countries with higher capital per person, absolute β – convergence (beta convergence) is said to take place. As most nations and regions exhibit widely varying patterns of savings and population growth rates, the foregoing is highly restrictive. However, conditional convergence is said to occur when there is evidence for convergence provided that saving and population growth rates and other types of national variance are controlled (Wolf, 1992). A third type of convergence is absolute σ – convergence (sigma convergence) which refers to the tendency of the dispersion of real per capita income levels to decrease over time. This can be seen in the case where $\sigma_{t+T} < \sigma_t$, where σ_t is the standard deviation over time of income across the particular observations. β – convergence is required for σ – convergence to exist, but can be had without having σ – convergence present.

Much of the growth literature estimates relationships via the traditional and well known Cobb-Douglas function. It has been shown by Barro and Sali-i-Martin (1995) that results similar to those generated via a Cobb-Douglas specification can be obtained through use of a production function taking a constant-elasticity-of-substitution (CES) form; however, this method is only appropriate if the elasticity of substitution between capital and labor is high. Arrow et al (1961) initially employed the CES approach. The distinguishing characteristic of the CES function is that it allows the value of the elasticity of substitution to be greater or less than unity. In Arrow's work, it was determined that given the particular data employed the test restriction imposed by a Cobb-Douglas functional form was significantly different from 1 in most cases and consequently an adequate explanation for the relationship at hand was not provided. Thus, the CES was particularly useful in that it enabled the elasticity of substitution to differ from unity and thus yield more insights into relationships among input variables.

The other functional form occasionally employed in the growth literature is the transcendental logarithmic function (translog). This form consists of a Taylor series expansion of an arbitrary function. Through its use one need not impose a priori restrictions as to the elasticity of inputs or for our case the determinants of average per-capita income growth. Despite this attractive feature, this approach has not been employed frequently by growth theorists.

Regional Growth Theories

Insights into sources of differentiation and its impact on economic growth and income convergence also may be derivable from theories of regional growth. These have never been welded to the work of either the neoclassical or more contemporary growth theorists because of the a-spatial nature of most British and American economic theory. From the 1950s to the 1960s major bodies of theory were developed to explain sub-national growth (Perloff et al, 1960). The principal means to organize information and data to explain the growth of regions were the "export base" and "sector" concepts.

Export base theory hypothesized that a primary contributor to the growth of a region was the export base of the region. Growth in this model is attributed to the response of industries within the region to demand outside of the region: as export activity increases income will increase through a multiplier process, and expenditure of this income will produce growth in non-exporting region-serving employment and income. The rate at which the region grows thus becomes a function of how effectively the export base responds to exogenous demand for exportable goods and services, and the magnitude of intra-regional multiplier effects.

In a classic study, Borts and Stein (1964) developed a neoclassical based model for the analysis of economic growth consistent with export base theory. They undertook an analysis of intrastate differences in the rate of growth of per capita income in the U.S. Using data for the periods 1880-1900, 1900-1920 and 1920-1950 they found that there was a positive relation between the growth in manufacturing and growth in per capita income. They found that convergence of per-capita income among the states was associated with the shifting of labor from low wage states to high wage states. Noted was a tendency toward factor price equalization, concluding that the rate of growth of per capita income was dependent upon the wage differential between agricultural and non-agricultural sectors as well as the fraction of the labor force employed in the lower wage sector (agriculture). In this work they introduced the idea now known as σ (sigma) convergence, and they concluded that low-wage regions will experience the highest rates of growth of capital, of the ratio of capital to labor, and of the growth of wages.

To test for σ − convergence the tendency for dispersion in per capita income to decline over time, Borts and Stein used the formulation:

$$Y/P = W_n \bullet L_n/P + W_a \bullet L_a/P + Q/P \qquad (2.13)$$

where W_n is average income of nonagricultural worker, W_a is the ratio of nonagricultural employment to population, is average income per agricultural worker, L_a/P is ratio of agricultural employment to population, Q/P is property income per capita and Y/P is personal income per capita. In this formulation, sigma convergence occurs when the dispersion of per capita income decreases as the portion of workers employed in the manufacturing sector increases.

Endogenous Growth Theory

As an alternative to the neoclassical growth formulation, in 1992 Barro and Sala-i-Martin, proposed an endogenous growth model. Their model began by postulating a neoclassical production function that possesses the quality of labor augmenting technology for the case of the i-th firm. Income in this model is a function of capital, labor and technology and is expressed mathematically as,

$$Y_i = F(K_i, A_i, L_i), \tag{2.14}$$

Li and *Ki* are the inputs conventionally found in the neo-classical production function, and *Ai* is an index of knowledge (technology) available to the firm. Technology is assumed to be labor augmenting so that a steady state exists when *Ai* is growing at a constant rate. What is significant is that a firm or an economy that increases its physical capital learns to simultaneously produce more efficiently. This is known as learning-by-doing or learning-by-investing. Thus, increases in capital stock lead to increases in knowledge and hence an increase in output. Critics have pointed out that this Barro Sala-i-Martin model is merely a more elaborate neoclassical formulation with the inclusion of technology and other factors, however externalities resulting from technology are static and technology is a public good. Since externalities are static there are no cumulative effects and thus there are no increasing returns to capital. In effect, this formulation, while including technology, does not significantly augment the productivity of input factors (Nelson, 1997; Davis, 1992).

Sector-growth theorists suggested the possibility of increasing returns several decades ago. Sector driven growth theory stems from the notion that increases in per capita income have been accompanied by a decline of the labor force employed in agriculture and an increase in that portion of the labor force employed in manufacturing and in support and service activities (Perloff et al, 1960). Changes in sector composition are seen as providing the engine of economic growth by increasing both the volume of economic activity and per capita income. In a typology reminiscent of Rostow's stages of economic growth, sector growth theorists developed a theory of developmental stages. In this typology, a region or city will initially be characterized by a self sufficient subsistence economy. A city will then experience growth through specialization in primary activities and interregional trade then by the introduction of primary industries, by a shifting to more diversified industry, and finally by specialization in certain tertiary industries for export of specialized goods and services.

This view was central to the work of Thompson (1965). In this work it is argued that the growth of a city can be best understood by the economic role the particular city has assumed, as reflected in the sectors that it has developed and the internal development of functions which allow it to serve as a regional center. Key to Thompson's argument is that a city that assumes the role of regional center grows at a greater rate and enjoys higher incomes and better prospects than less able or less adaptable urban centers because of the self transforming process unlocked by scale and status. Researchers did not pick up and build upon these ideas, however, and an opportunity thus was missed for regional theory to become an acknowledged part of modern endogenous growth theory until Krugman (1991) proclaimed his 'new economic geography'. This 'new economic geography' is not new at all, and consists of sharpening and bringing to the attention of the economics profession approaches which had been employed by a number of empirical researchers for many years. In his work Krugman (1995) integrates several older approaches and then augments them with microeconomic foundations now possible with advances in modeling and computational techniques.

Krugman integrates central place theory, market potential and the idea of circular and cumulative causation, arguing that cities are a result of growth and specialization, and result specifically from increasing returns. The notion of cumulative causation, has its roots in the work of Myrdal (1957). The principal idea of cumulative causation is that urban agglomerations provide a large market which attracts new industries which in turn enlarge the local market. Concentrations of urban activity can stem from accidents of history, but whatever the cause, concentration leads to specialization, and specialization leads to increasing returns. With increasing returns it is advantageous to further concentrate the production of each good at a few locations. There is thus a tendency for cities to specialize in production. An example cited of this tendency is the concentration of United States manufacturing in an area known as the "manufacturing belt" roughly a parallelogram defined by Green Bay, St. Louis, Baltimore and Portland Maine (Krugman, 1991).

The 'new' growth theory that fully incorporates concepts of endogeniety and positive feedback had its start in a paper by Paul Romer (1986). Romer enlarged the idea of capital used in growth theory to include the well developed idea of human capital, and in doing so discovered that the laws of diminishing returns may not apply. Unlike the neoclassical model, the new growth theory endogenizes technological progress within the model, making possible positive feedback mechanisms that result in divergent rather than convergent growth.

In the framework developed by Romer, technology plays a central role in the process of growth. The benefits that accrue as a result of technological advance are not static but tend to accumulate. This generates dynamic externalities and agglomeration effects, which further strengthen the role of technology. Very importantly, in this framework, technology can induce increasing returns to particular factor inputs. Technology such as enhancement of human capital via university training, industrial research and development, process improvements, etc., can generate increasing returns and a concomitant increase in income and economic growth.

Consequently, unlike the neoclassical growth model, endogenous growth theory predicts divergence in economic growth and performance. That technological progress is discontinuous, and that there are significant spillover effects due to this progress, leads to growth being discontinuous as well increasing due to the increasing returns to capital. Technological progress is broadly defined. It may find its prime mover in the form of human capital accumulation. That generates knowledge spillover's which serve as an impetus to economic activity and growth (Romer, 1990). However, the accumulation of productive capital in various physical forms such as new equipment or research facilities may also result in growth-generating economic activity. Growth may also result from the agglomeration of particular industries within particular regions or cities (Krugman, 1991). That technological advance stems from disparate and not omnipresent sources inevitably leads to divergence. For example, the wide divergence in human capital around the world is thought to explain the persistent gap in income levels between developed and less developed nations (Romer, 1993).

Barro and Sala-i-Martin (1995) formally summarize the model developed by Romer as follows:

$$Y_i = F(K_i, A_i L_i) \tag{2.15}$$

Li and *Ki* are the standard inputs labor and capital, respectively. *Ai* is an index of knowledge available to the firm. While appearing no different than the neoclassical version they presented in 1992, this model assumes that an increase in capital stock leads to an increase in knowledge. This process reflects the idea developed by Arrow that knowledge and productivity gains come from investment. The second assumption is that knowledge is a public good that any firm can readily access at zero cost. This implies that knowledge spreads throughout an economy. By adding the assumptions of learning-by-doing and knowledge spillover's, A_i can be replaced by K. This permits the production function to be expressed as:

$$Y_i = F(K_i, K \bullet L_i), \tag{2.16}$$

With L_i and K constant, diminishing returns to K_i are faced. Yet, if each producer expands K_i, then K rises and provides a spillover benefit that raises productivity throughout the economy. Since the equation above is homogenous of degree one in K_i and K for a given L_i, there are constant returns to scale. According to Barro and Sala-i-Martin (1995), this constancy of social returns to capital will yield endogenous growth. The firm's profit function is written as:

$$L_i \bullet [f(k_i, K) - (r + \delta) \bullet k_i - w], \tag{2.17}$$

Here $r + \delta$ is the rental price of capital, and w is the wage rate. It should be noted that rental price of capital can also be viewed as the opportunity cost of capital. These factor prices are taken as given. Also, it is assumed in the model that each firm is sufficiently small so as that its contribution to the capital stock is negligible and thus treats K as given (Romer, 1986). The usual conditions of profit maximization and the zero profit condition imply:

$$\partial y_i / \partial k_i = f_1(k_i, K) = r + \delta, \tag{2.18}$$

$$\partial Y_i / \partial L_i = f(k_i, K) - k_i \bullet f1(k_i, K) = w \tag{2.19}$$

Here $f_1(\bullet, \bullet)$ is the partial derivative of $f(k_i, K) = w$ with respect to its first argument, k_i which is the private marginal product of capital. This neglects the contribution of k_i to K and to knowledge. It is also assumed that all firms make the same choices, thus $k_i = k$ and $K=kL$. Given that $f(k_i, K)$ is homogenous of degree one in k_i and K, the average product of capital can be expressed as:

$$f(k_i, K / k_i = \tilde{f}(K / k_i) = \tilde{f}(L), \tag{2.20}$$

Where $\tilde{f}(L) > 0$ and $\tilde{f}'(L) < 0$. This average product of capital is invariant with respect to due to positive spillover effects and learning-by-doing removing the presence of diminishing returns.

The average product increases with the size of the labour force L, which in turn leads to scale effects. The private marginal product of capital is expressed as:

$$f_1(k_i, K) = \tilde{f}(L) - L \bullet \tilde{f}(L). \tag{2.21}$$

The private marginal product of capital is less than the average product, $\tilde{f}(L)$ and is invariant with respect to k. This also implies that the private marginal product of capital is increasing in L due to $\tilde{f}'(L) < 0$.

There has been some question as to the extent of the novelty of endogenous growth theory. The critique of the new growth theory rests on the assertion that since the late 1950s the majority of formal neo-classical models did in fact recognize technological advance as the motive force behind economic growth. The limitation cited as a feature of endogenous growth models is a lack of clarity as to the sources of technological advance. This critique is primarily confined to those engaged in the development of theory. Nelson (1997) argues that the various facets have long been understood and documented by empirical scholars. Moreover, the majority of the new growth models are in essence as simple as the traditional neo-classical models, save for the treatment of firms and the concomitant spread of innovation. The telling limitation, according to Nelson, is that the firms are treated in a fairly simplified way since there is no realistic treatment of institutions which can have a significant effect on the process of growth. Institutional variation in the new growth theory is essentially subsumed under the assumption of a competitive or a monopolistically competitive market.

Other researchers have turned their attention to different national institutions and their role in economic growth. Gilson (1993) examines the role of financial systems. More employable for the present study is the work of Nelson (1993), which examines the role of universities in national growth. While all cities in the United States can be assumed to share a common financial system, there is a range of variation in the number and type of universities within the various metropolitan areas of the United States.

Public Expenditure and Economic Growth

Few growth theorists include government expenditures as a variable in their models. In the present study government expenditure is utilized as a test variable to examine its impact under the various growth formulations. Borts and Stein (1964) noted that to some degree law and government regulation are deliberately employed to stimulate the growth of some regions at the expense of others. They noted the need for the application of standards for an efficient growth process in the nation, and explored the extent to which public expenditures could satisfy these goals. The principal theoretical impetus for including government expenditure is that since the Second World War, empirical studies indicate that economic growth is primarily attributable to increases in productivity and not increases in inputs (Denison, 1968). It follows, then that government expenditures to some extent can serve as a proxy for investments in physical and social infrastructure or social overhead capital that serves to augment productivity (Rostow, 1954). Physical infrastructure can take the form of investment in various forms of capital which can augment productivity such as highways, airports and port facilities. Similarly, investment in social infrastructure such as child nutrition and education directly contribute to enhancing the well being and ultimately the productivity of human beings.

In recent years, the work of Aschauer (1989) and Munnel (1990) has stimulated a good deal of discussion with regard to the role and efficacy of public expenditure. Both of these authors utilized a Cobb-Douglas formulation in their approach with Aschauer utilizing national aggregates and Munnel a regional analysis. Their studies were exceptions to the greater body of literature exploring the role of public expenditures and economic activity. They are exceptional in that both found that public expenditures had significant impacts on levels of economic output. The balance of the literature finds that public expenditures have at most a modest impact on economic performance.

Aschauer sought to verify whether public expenditure was productive by examining the relationship between aggregate productivity and stock and flow government spending variables. He discovered that in fact non-military public infrastructure contributed significantly to productivity growth and that military capital (military bases, facilities, etc.) bore little relationship to productivity. Expenditure flows both military and non-military were far less significant in affecting productivity. Thus, non-military investment in capital stock leads to increases in productivity.

Munnel examined the effect of public infrastructure on regional economic performance. Employing a state by state comparison in the United States, Munnel concluded that states that had invested more in infrastructure tended to higher levels of output, private investment and employment growth and that public investment occurs prior to increases in economic activity. This study was critiqued in that levels rather than growth rates were employed. Also, subsequent efforts to replicate the study using dis-aggregated data proved to be unsuccessful. Further, the issue of causality has been raised in this work. It is unclear if higher income areas generate higher tax revenues and their concomitant higher public expenditures. Thus, higher incomes may be generating higher public investment and not vice versa. There is thus some question as to conclusions drawn from this work of the extent of the effect of government spending on income growth.

Exemplifying the work of neoclassical analysts, Crihfield and Panggabean (1995) examined the productive effects of public infrastructure in metropolitan areas utilizing the estimates of public capital stocks developed by Munnel (1990), Holtz-Eakin (1994) and the National Cooperative Highway Research Program (1991). Combining these infrastructure measures with data for the states and 282 metropolitan areas and estimating the standard Solow growth model, they found that public infrastructure had a modest effect on factor markets and an even smaller impact on growth in per-capita income. This is consistent with the work of Holtz-Eakin and the finding that public infrastructure investment will not generate above-market returns. Other researchers, such as Mila and McGuire (1992) and Schwab (1981, 1991), appear to confirm a negligible role for public capital, but Berndt and Hansson (1992) and Manuneas (1994) demur, finding that public capital and public expenditures contribute significantly to economic output and economic growth.

Enough questions are raised by this body of research that government expenditure variables are included in the tests of both the neoclassical and the endogenous growth hypotheses.

Issues Surrounding Convergence

According to Kim (1997) and Quah (1993,1996,1996b) there are issues surrounding the usefulness of the notion of convergence. In particular, the usefulness of the notion of conditional convergence relative to absolute convergence is questioned, as is the relevance of β – convergence compared to σ -convergence (Kim, 1998). Quah argues that the distinction between absolute and conditional convergence is not useful in determining cross sectional changes in income distribution over time. However, the purpose of traditional growth theory is not to test the distribution of income but rather the rate at which incomes converge and the effect of certain determinants on the rate of income convergence. Neoclassical growth theorists defend their approach from critiques such as that of Quah, by noting that tests of conditional convergence are not meant to test income distributions around the globe. The approach is intended to test for decreasing returns to capital, and whether growth patterns favor neoclassical growth theory instead of endogenous growth theory (Kim, 1997).

With regard to the usefulness of β -convergence in testing the rate of income convergence, Quah argues that β convergence yields no insight into a distribution's behavior and that regressions on a cross section are representative of only average behavior and not that of an entire distribution. Quah also takes issue with the neoclassical concern of whether β -convergence implies σ -convergence. He argues that it is irrelevant, as the primary focus should remain on σ -convergence. Using the notion of Galton's fallacy of regression toward the mean, he shows that β -convergence does not provide an indication of convergence or divergence. On the other hand, the neoclassicists, argue that conditional β -convergence can be had even while there is increasing dispersion of world incomes because the two notions are different (Kim, 1997). They argue that Galton's fallacy does not apply to neoclassical growth theory since the concept of convergence has it that it is the "tendency of weak teams to rebound toward the mean and of champions to revert to mediocrity" (Barro, 1995). The neoclassicists argue further (Sala-i-Martin, 1996a), that σ − convergence measures the variation of world income distribution over time, whereas β -convergence captures the movement of individual economies within a particular distribution (Kim, 1997). Yet, according to Quah (1996, 1996), the neoclassical formulation of convergence can not capture the actual mobility of particular economies and is misleading (Kim, 1997). What the neoclassical economists have actually found is a group or club pattern. Quah, refers to this as 'club convergence' which according to him in reality indicates divergence. The existence of divergence according to Quah is due to conditional convergence not including the phenomenon of polarization. In transnational studies of convergence of world incomes dispersion remains constant or increases over time.

The key issue is that movements of real per capita gross domestic product generate a negative relationship due to movements in GDP levels. This phenomenon is not accounted for via conditional β -convergence (Kim, 1997).

Other researchers, have also questioned the ability to generate accurate measures of convergence (Durlauf, 1996b). Some have also measured the ability to infer measures of welfare from rates of convergence (Baumol, 1988; De Long, 1988). In general, many researchers advocate caution in inferences made from convergence results and urge attention to the methods and data employed in testing the convergence phenomenon.

3 Empirical Tests of the Convergence Hypothesis

Many tests have been performed of both absolute and conditional convergence hypothesis using cross-sectional, time series and pooled data from different nations. The results are neither strongly consistent nor clear. Varying model specifications, variable selection, sample size, sample period and data sources seem to produce widely varying results. The bulk of the studies examine convergence at the national level, but there are a few studies which have sought to test different versions of the hypothesis of the convergence hypothesis employing sub-national data. These studies differ from those undertaking cross national convergence not only in the data utilized but in some of the key assumptions underlying the different growth and convergence theories.

Neoclassical Theory Based Findings

Barro and Sali-i-Martin (1991, 1991a, 1992), undertook tests of the convergence hypothesis for 47 of the component states of the United States for regions of Europe, and for the component prefectures of Japan. Using data for 1880-1990 for the United States, convergence was tested using the following formulation:

$$(1/T) \bullet \log(y_{it} / y_{i,t_-} T) = a - [\log(y_{i,t_-T})] \bullet [(1 - e^{-\beta T}) / T] + \textit{other}$$
$$\textit{variables} \tag{3.1}$$

where per capita income in state i at the start of the data interval divided by the overall consumer price index, T is the length of the interval, and the 'other variables' consist of regional dummies and other structural measures which the authors employ to control for conditional convergence. The different equations were estimated by non-linear least squares.

The results for the United States show β -convergence in a basic neoclassical model and in two more elaborate models using control variables that include employment sector composition, and regional dummies. The rates of convergence for the long sample were .017 for the basic model, .018 and .022 respectively for the equation with sector composition and with regional dummies. For all cases the estimated coefficient is significantly positive, indicating β -convergence for seven of the nine sub-periods (Barro, 1990).

Barro and Sala-i-Martin also examined the phenomenon of σ -convergence. The dispersion of income among the American states declined from .54 in 1880 to .33 in 1920, but increased to .40 in 1930. In 1940, dispersion fell to .35, .24 in 1950, .21 in 1960, .17 in 1970 and .19 in 1988 (Barro, 1992).

In analyzing 90 regions for eight European countries, Barro and Sala-i-Martin found income convergence did not show the pattern of the U.S. Rather, in the European case, the β coefficient is unstable. The differences in convergence among both countries and sub regions was significant. The rates of convergence range from .0224 for Germany to .0182 for Spain. Utilizing data for Japanese prefectures, for the years 1930-1990 the pattern of β -convergence was analyzed. Nonlinear least squares was used to obtain estimates of the convergence coefficient β. The rate of convergence for the Japanese prefectures was found to be .01 employing a basic formulation, .0232 and .0312 employing models including regional dummies and that including employment sector composition and regional dummies, respectively.

Crihfield and Panggabean undertook an application of the Solow-Swan model to the question of whether growth has been accompanied by convergence across U.S. cities in 1995. Utilizing disaggregated data from a cross section of 282 U.S. metropolitan areas for the period 1960-1982 they found that real per capita incomes converged across U.S. metropolitan areas at the rate of about 6% per year during the 1960-1977 period. It was also found that the rate of convergence slowed over time. The model indicated that there was little reason to conclude that government investment contributed to growth in per capita income from 1960-1982. Thus neoclassical predictions held only under fairly restrictive conditions. They concluded that only if these other conditions are properly identified and controlled will there be evidence of convergence: convergence is 'conditional' upon these other sources of differentiation.

Other neoclassical studies have used proxies to test for the presence of technology augmentation or the deleterious effect of government expenditure, it could better be allocated by market processes. In an examination of productivity and income growth and convergence, Morrison and Schwartz (1996), extended the work of Munnel and examined the effect of state infrastructure investment and productive performance of manufacturing. Counter to the findings of Crihfield et al, Morrison and Schwartz, found that infrastructure investment provides a significant return to manufacturing firms and aids in productivity growth. These findings were tempered with the additional finding that net benefits of infrastructure investment depend upon the costs of infrastructure investment and the relative growth rates of output and infrastructure investment (Morrison and Schwartz, 1996).

Endogenous Growth Theory Test Findings

To date, there is no direct example of research employing an endogenous growth formulation to examine the determinants of income convergence/divergence for cities and/or metropolitan areas. A number of empirical studies have sought to employ an endogenous growth model to test for convergence/divergence employing cross-national data.

The paucity of empirical research and significant findings has been noted by Pack (1992). While endogenous growth theory has a clear intuitive appeal, empirical research that can be classified as being strictly within the rubric of endogenous growth theory is very limited. Despite theoretical breakthroughs, even the empirical work of Romer is viewed by many as not altogether convincing or significant (Pack, 1995). This paucity of research is particularly true with respect to sub-national data.

An analysis carried out by Sherwood-Call (1996) investigated the characteristics of income and its growth and convergence for the fifty American states during the 1980s. While the research did not examine the determinants of growth, it did seek to ascertain the rate of income convergence across the states. What was found was that incomes had diverged among the U.S. states over the decade. While the approach and methodology can be classified as neither strictly neoclassical nor endogenous, it confirms what an endogenous growth model would predict given the heterogeneities of growth determining variables among the states.

The idea that returns to private technological innovation are increasing has been applied in examining the growth of cities. Glaeser et al (1992) employ the idea of knowledge spillover's as a possible determinant of growth in cities. Their approach, rather than examining general determinants of income (as in the present study), examines the industry composition of cities. They compare three approaches to explain economic growth. In particular, the role of technological spillovers is stressed. It is argued that since both knowledge and technological spillovers are particularly effective in cities, data for 170 cities between 1956 and 1987 are used to test the effects of varying degrees of industrial sector specialization on industrial employment growth. Of particular importance is to determine whether knowledge and technological spillover's are more prolific within or between different industries. Ultimately, Glaeser et al seek to test the hypothesis that cities characterized by highly specialized economies fare better that those cities whose economies are more diffuse or less specialized. The work indicates that employment growth, and by extension city growth, is most enhanced in cities characterized by a diverse group of industries. This is consistent with the work of Jacobs (1968) which argued that diversity contributes more to city growth than does industrial specialization, a conclusion which seems to run counter to the central tenets of Krugman's 'new' economic geography. This results, Glaeser et al say, because technological and knowledge spillover's occur at a greater rate among cities that show industrial heterogeneity than those exhibiting industrial specialization do.

4 Research Hypothesis and Models Tested

Clearly there is much that has to be resolved about the relevance of neoclassical and endogenous growth theories at the sub-national level, and about related notions of income convergence and divergence. The principal hypotheses tested in this study are whether the economic growth of U.S. metropolitan areas, as measured by growth in real per capita income, can be most satisfactorily explained using the traditional Solow-Swan neoclassical growth model or via more comprehensive models that incorporate the new endogenous growth theory. In the case of neoclassical growth, tests are completed for both absolute and conditional types of β – convergence, as well as for σ – convergence.

Testing for Absolute β – Convergence

The first step is to test for absolute β – convergence employing the basic Barro neoclassical growth model. The process here is straightforward and is merely a replication of Barro's 1991 work on the U.S. states employing MSA data. While seemingly a mere exercise, this is a useful step: it can be determined whether income convergence for the U.S. cities occurred during the time frame in manner consistent with what neoclassical theory would predict (convergence increasing over time) or exhibits some other tendency. Step one thus involves the test of:

Research Hypothesis 1 : The growth rate of income decreases as income increases. The level of absolute β -convergence decreases over time when controlling for initial levels of income.

The first step as indicated by Research Hypothesis 1, is thus to examine the process of convergence. Here we take the Barro and Sala-i-Martin equation:

$$\log(y_{i1}/y_{i,t-1}) = a - (1-e^{-\beta}) \bullet \log(y_{i,t-1}) + u_{it}, \tag{4.1}$$

The subscript t denotes year, the subscript i denotes the MSA, and is income for a given year and MSA. The theoretical implication is that the intercept term, which is equal to $x + (1 - e^{-\beta}) \bullet [\log(yi^*) + x \bullet (t-1)]yi^*$ is the steady state level of y_y. It is assumed that the random variable u_{it} has a mean with a value 0 and varianceσ^2_{ut} distributed independent of log $(y_{i,t-1}), u_{jt}$ for $j \neq i$ and lagged disturbances. In this formulation, the random disturbances reflect unexpected changes in production or preferences. The specification also means that the time trend and steady state are the same for all MSA's. In effect if a is the same for all MSA's and β is > 0, it can be said that poor cities have tended to grow faster than richer cites over the period of interest.

Estimation is undertaken via ordinary least squares (OLS). The first step will be to examine convergence for the periods 1970-1975, 1975-1980, 1980-1985, 1985-1990 and for the entire 1970-1990 period. The form of the model used to estimate convergence thus becomes:

$$(1/T) \bullet \log(y_{it} / y_{i,t-T}) = a - [\log(y_{i,t-T})] \bullet [(1 - e^{-\beta T})/T] + e_i \qquad (4.2)$$

where y_i is per-capita income in MSA is at the beginning of each time interval, T is the length of the interval. Whereas Barro divided this value by the CPI appropriate to the time interval, our data have already been adjusted to constant dollar values and thus this step is unnecessary.

In the second step, involving a more elaborate testing procedure, the primary issue is whether convergence coefficients have negative signs in model specifications that include the several endogenous growth variables, human capital, technology, Carnegie I research universities, capital investment, government expenditures and unionization. The issue to be examined is whether there is a significant negative relationship on the conditional β-coefficient. This leads to the second research hypothesis as is stated as follows:

Research hypothesis 2: The coefficient on the initial level of MSA per capita income (conditional β-convergence coefficient) shows a negative sign when tested using the growth rate of the independent variables.

Hypothesis 2 thus focuses on whether the neo-classical idea of growth is relevant to an understanding of metropolitan area income growth by examining the phenomenon of conditional convergence, the tendency for growth rates to converge when controlling for other factors. Of particular importance is the effect of human capital and physical capital investment-the two main explanatory variables in the neoclassical growth model. The speed with which convergence occurs is an important component of this test.

In the second step, the neoclassical growth model is expanded to include other structural variables, permitting examination of the idea of conditional convergence. The model for conditional convergence is tested for the periods 1970-1975, 1975-1980, 1980-1985, 1985-1990 and for the entire 1970-1990 period. The limitation of this work is that it focuses primarily on the convergence parameter and does not provide any insight as to the determinants of income convergence.

The neoclassical growth equation to be estimated to test hypothesis 2 is:

$$YG = \beta 0 + \beta 1 y0 + \beta 2 capinv + \beta 3 capaug + \beta 4 union + \beta 5 pop + \beta 6 tax + \beta 7 humcap + e_i \tag{4.3}$$

The dependent variable YG, is estimated as growth in per capita MSA income, *capinv* is capital investment in new equipment, *Humcap* is level of human capital either high school or college completion (or both) rates by MSA, *Union* is rates of unionization (this to test freedom of factor market function) and *Pop* is population, the reason here is that one is assuming that the size of the labor force is a function of the population. *Pop* serves also as a proxy for the effect of agglomeration economies, that is the tendency of larger centers of population to realize economies of scale in production and hence higher levels and growth rates of income. *Tax* is the statewide average property tax rate, this is applied as in other empirical research to determine if taxes have a negative effect on income growth. The coefficient of interest is $\beta 1$, since here we see if there is convergence and if so at what rate. To appropriately estimate the process of convergence, all non-dychotomous variables are measured as growth rates and not levels. This will preclude the likelihood of spurious results brought on as a consequence of downward sloping bias. The rate of growth is obtained by taking the difference between the initial year and the following year and calculating it as percentage change from year t to year t+1.

MSA and time dummy variables are added to the model to control for time and city effects. Also added is the variable *capaug*, which denotes the presence of a Carnegie Class I research university in a particular MSA. This fixed effects model assumes that the intercept varies over time t units and/or across N cross sectional units (Kennedy, 1991; Green, 1992). Typically, (N-1)+(T-1) dummies can be used. The dummy coefficients for time and for cross sectional units are inserted to allow the shifting of the regression line arising from unknown temporal or spatial factors. The fixed effects model estimated is thus:

$$YG = \beta 0 + \beta 1y0 + \beta 2capinv + \beta 3humcap + \beta 4union + \beta 5pop$$
$$+ \beta 6tax + \beta 7capaug + \beta 8msad + \beta 9time + e$$
(4.4)

A variation of hypothesis 2 is theoretically distinct in that government expenditures can be viewed as a source of institutional variation amongst the different MSAs. In this variant, the assumption is made that differing levels of funds obtained from the federal government reflect different cultural and political proclivities and prowess among the different MSAs.

Research hypothesis 2a: The coefficient on the initial level of MSA per capita income (conditional β -convergence coefficient) will show a negative sign when tested using the growth rate of independent variables augmented by government expenditures.

Both 4.3 and 4.4 will be estimated with the addition of the government expenditure variable βgov. For each of the models described above, tests for σ − convergence are undertaken utilizing the cross sectional standard deviation for the log of per capita income for the 231 MSAs during the period of interest.

The alternative to hypothesis 2 is that the coefficient on the initial level of per capita MSA income shows a positive sign when it is tested using the growth rate of the independent variables, including human capital, physical capital, technology, government expenditures and population:

Research hypothesis 3: The coefficient on the initial level of MSA per capita income (conditional β -convergence coefficient) will show a positive sign when tested using endogenous growth variables.

This is the case of the endogenous growth model. First a basic model will first be estimated. Here an index of technology via the *Tech* variable is introduced directly into the model.

$$Yg = \beta 0 + \beta 1y + \beta 2capinv + \beta 3humcap + \beta 4capaug + \beta 5pop \\ + \beta 6tech + e \tag{4.5}$$

Yg is growth in per capita income, *Y* is income in base period, *capinv* is capital investment, *humcap* is human capital, *capaug* is capital augmentation (to get at the idea of learning by doing). In this specification, dummy variables for MSA and Year are used to control for time and City effects thus allowing for the determination of the effect over the entire cross section on income of the several independent variables that is not due to the heterogeneities of time and place. Again, the model is estimated using rates of growth and compared to one employing levels.

   A more elaborate version of the endogenous growth model will be estimated including the sectoral variables. This is done to include theoretically distinct basis of contemporary endogenous growth models with the ideas of regional science described previously. The regional growth theory model estimated is:

$$Yg = \beta 0 + \beta 1y + \beta 2capinv + \beta 3humcap + \beta 4capaug + \beta 5pop \\ + \beta 6serv + \beta 7manuf + \beta 8tech + e \tag{4.6}$$

To test for the effect of government/public expenditures the government expenditures variable is incorporated into each of the models. A vital component in the evaluation of neoclassical growth theory is to test for the presence of σ -convergence, i.e. whether the dispersion of per capita income among the MSAs declines over time, so a third hypothesis is formulated.

Research hypothesis 4: The standard deviation of the log of per capita income declines over time.

Tests for the process of σ -convergence are estimated as follows:

$$\log(y_{it}/y_{i,t-1}) = a - (1 - e^{-\beta}) \bullet \log(y_{i,t-1}) + u_{it} \qquad (4.7)$$

Here the subscript t denotes the particular year, and i denotes the MSA. σ_t^2 is cross MSA variance of $\log(y_{it})$ at time t. The properties of the disturbance term u_{it} implies that σ_t^2 evolves over time in accordance with:

$$\sigma_t^2 = e - 2\beta \bullet \sigma_{t-1}^2 + \sigma_{ut}^2 \qquad (4.8)$$

In drawing from earlier regional science based growth theory, the idea of sector led growth is an interesting contribution. To augment the neoclassical and endogenous growth formulations, the possibility of sector led growth will be tested, by examining whether the relative shares of manufacturing and service employment have the effect of reducing the dispersion of incomes among MSAs:

Research hypothesis 5: The standard deviation of the log of per capita income declines as a function of employment sector composition.

The testing of this hypothesis is as follows:

$$\log(y_{ir}/y_{i,r-1}) = a - (1 - e^{-\beta}) \bullet \log(y_{i,r-1}) + u_{ir} \qquad (4.9)$$

Here the subscript r denotes the ratio of manufacturing to service employment, for a particular year. Convergence thus is a function of the change of the manufacturing to service ratio.

5 Variable Selection and Data Development

Variable Selection and Utilization

The present work differs from most earlier applications of growth models, in two important respects. In earlier applications, the data employed have typically been cross national. Where nations are the unit of analysis, limitations of factor mobility have to be acknowledged since growth theory assumes mobility of the factors of production. To compensate, these earlier works have therefore included independent measures of the openness of economies. In the present case, it can be assumed that there is a much greater degree of factor mobility among the units of observation (metropolitan areas), obviating the need for measures of market openness. Otherwise, variable selection and inclusion is guided by prior attempts to test neoclassical and endogenous models, to build in sectoral differentiation, and to incorporate institutional differences such as the role of government.

Data Sources

The unit of observation for this study is the Standard Metropolitan Statistical Area (SMSA) as determined by the U.S. Department of Commerce. There were 277 of these areas in 1977. The time frame is 1970 through 1990. While data are relatively available for most of these MSAs a number were deleted because consistent information was unavailable over the entire time span. The total number of MSAs with complete data was 232. Thus, the data set employed for this study includes 21 years for 232 MSAs or 4872 observations. The MSAs that where deleted were primarily small, for example MSAs in the state of Connecticut for which data on manufacturing capital and employment is not released due to disclosure rules or for considerations of national security.

The variable used for income is money income per capita, converted to constant 1982 dollars using the consumer price index (Table 5.1). The nominal dollar amount is the estimated average amount per person of total money income received during a given calendar year for all persons residing within a particular jurisdiction. Total money income is defined by the U.S. Department of Commerce Bureau of the Census as the sum of wage or salary income, net non-farm self employment income, interest, dividends, net rental income, social security and railroad retirement income, public assistance, and all other regularly received income. What this measure does not include is income to juridical persons. These estimates are based on the decennial census and are updated by the Internal Revenue Service and the U.S. Department of Commerce Bureau of Economic Analysis (BEA). The source for SMSA population resides in U.S. Department of Commerce, Bureau of the Census, State and Metropolitan Area Data Book, various years. Sources for metropolitan total personal income include U.S. Department of Commerce, Bureau of the Census, *Survey of Current Business*, U.S. Department of Commerce, Bureau of the Census, *State and Metropolitan Area Data Book*; and U.S. Department of Commerce, Bureau of the Census, *County and City Data Book*.

Table 5.1 Consumer Price Index Deflators*

1970	2.574
1971	2.446
1972	2.391
1973	2.251
1974	2.029
1975	1.859
1976	1.757
1977	1.649
1978	1.532
1979	1.380
1980	1.215
1981	1.098
1982	1.000
1983	1.003
1984	0.961
1985	0.928
1986	0.913
1987	0.880
1988	0.846
1989	0.807
1990	0.766

*Value in 1982 Dollars

Source: U.S. Bureau of Labor Statistics, Survey of Current Business

The relative shares of manufacturing and service employment are obtained from the U.S. Bureau of the Census, *County Business Patterns,* various. The classification of employees is broad and is based on the 1972 edition of the Standard Industrial Classification (SIC) Manual. New capital expenditures for manufacturing will be used as a proxy for capital. These data are available by SMSA in U.S. Department of Commerce, Bureau of the Census, Census of Manufactures, Area Statistics and Subject Series. There is a limitation to the consistency of the service sector employment data. The types and number of occupations classified broadly as belonging to the service sector changed after the 1980 decennial census. Consequently, analysis employing this approach will be confined to the 1980-1990 data, for which a consistent and up to date data source exists.

The data for government expenditures consist of the totals for federal funds and grants as well as total expenditures. This data is prepared by the Bureau of the Census and includes data from the Federal Assistance Award System, Federal Procurement Data System, Office of Personnel Management, Department of Defense, included also is information on payments to local governments by federal agencies. The source of this data is the U.S. Bureau of the Census, *Consolidated Federal Funds Report* (CFFR), various years. Similarly, for public capital stocks, fixed reproducible wealth of the United States 1925-95, can be used, and public sector investment and taxation are obtainable from the *City and County Data Book,* Government Expenditures and *Statistical Abstract of the U.S.,* various years.

The standard proxy for human capital is the percentage of persons 25 years and older who have completed college, that is that percentage of the population within a particular MSA that holds a baccalaureate degree. Data are available by county in the *State and Metropolitan Area Data Book,* and *County and City Data Book.* The proxy for human capital augmentation and quality will be the presence of one or more of the nation's 88 principal universities as determined by their designation as 'Carnegie Class I'.

The best sources of unionization data are found at the state level: the percentage of a state's labor force having membership in a union, available from the U.S. Department of Commerce, Bureau of the Census, *Statistical Abstract of the United States,* various. For a technology index, estimates of the numbers of engineers and scientists per MSA are used. This proxy is intended to approximate the idea of increasing returns possible via technological knowledge. This proxy is employed under the assumption that scientists and engineers contribute to the effective and efficient use of resources. The source for this data is U.S. Department of Labor, Bureau of Labor Statistics (BLS), *Geographic Profile of Employment and Unemployment,* annual. And U.S. Department of Commerce, Economics and Statistics Administration, *State and Metropolitan Area Data Book,* Various. For taxes, the average property tax rate for each state is used. The source for this is U.S. Department of Commerce, *Census of Governments,* Various.

Since unionization and tax rate data are only readily available at the state level. In the estimation process this poses some problems in that a number of MSA span two or more states. In these cases, a simple arithmetic mean was obtained for both the rate of unionization and tax rates per year for each of the MSA's which occupy two or more states.

An issue facing this type of research is that data, while available for most years in most series are not available for all years. In the case of those variables for which data was not available for a particular year, a non-linear spline was utilized to interpolate estimates of the data not available. In Appendix B, where the data are presented, those values that have been interpolated via the non-linear spline are presented in bold face type.

Only one data set is used. Tests of the different theoretical approaches all employ the same data, varying only in the modifications called for by the requirements of a given theoretical specification. The complete list of variables is shown in table 5.2.

Table 5.2 Summary List of Variables

MSA	232 Metropolitan Statistical Areas
Y	Per Capita Personal Income
Capinv	Expenditures for Manufacturing Capital Equipment
Pop	Population
Humcap	Percentage of Population with a Bachelors Degree
Union	Statewide Percentage of Work force in Unions
Time	Year
Capaug	Presence of Carnegie I Research University
Manuf	Number of Workers Employed in Manufacturing
Serv	Number of Workers Employed in Service Sector
SectG	Ratio of Manufacturing to Service Employment
Tech	Number of Workers in Research, Engineering, Management
Tax	State level rate of property tax
Gov	Total Federal Government Expenditures Per MSA

Estimation Issues

The models are calibrated using variables measured using growth rates. In Appendix B these results are compared with results employing variables measured with levels, because issues have arisen regarding the effects of the measurement of independent variables in prior empirical work. Kim (1997) finds that the use of level variables in neoclassical formulations that employ pooled-time-series or cross sectional data is likely to lead to a downward sloping bias. This occurs because the relationship between initial levels of income and the levels of control variables may be positive even while the growth rates of the control variables show an opposite relationship with the result that the convergence coefficients have negative signs. This in turn, "may be the source of the constant predicted 2% convergence rate that was found by neoclassical growth theorists, because the levels of control variables do not change dramatically within the 30 to 40 years for which most data sets are available" (Kim, 1997). This possibility is addressed by using the growth form of the variables.

A corollary difficulty with the use of the level form of data is that it is likely to posses a unit root problem. A unit root problem is said to exist when there is a violation of the standard assumption that the means and variances of the variables are well defined constants and independent of time. Applications of unit root tests have shown that these assumptions are not satisfied by a large number of economic time-series data. Variables whose means and variances change over time are known as non-stationary or unit root variables. If the means and variances of the unit root variables change over time, all the computed statistics in a regression model using these variables are also time dependent and thus fail to converge to their true values as the sample size increases (Rao, 1994). The data set contains twenty-one year's (21) and is not likely to be reliable, but tests are undertaken to test particularly for stationarity. The dependent variable and all the independent variables are tested. The results are provided in Appendix C.

6 Empirical Results

The empirical results are presented in accordance with the five hypotheses posited in Chapter 4. The results presented begin with those of the absolute β – convergence hypothesis and continue with the results of the conditional β -convergence hypothesis tested using growth rate forms of the independent variables. These are followed by tests of the endogenous growth model, and then augmented with sector components as determinants of income growth. Models using level forms of the variables estimated for annual cross sections for both neoclassical and endogenous formulations are presented in Appendix B. For the more elaborate formulations employing ordinary least squares with fixed effects estimation the first year of the relevant period is taken as the base year and the reference MSA (Abilene, TX) was arbitrarily selected as it is the first on the data set. The values of the coefficients for the 231 MSA's utilized as well as those of the component years are not listed as they would make the presentation of the results extraordinarily cumbersome and would be of marginal value in further illustration of time and place effects on the process of income convergence or divergence.

Absolute β – Convergence Results

The first test was that of absolute beta convergence as proposed by neoclassical growth theory and as indicated in equation 4.2. The estimation proceeded via ordinary least squares (OLS) and included dummy variables to capture time effects. As is shown in table 6.1 there is evidence for divergence rather than convergence (the sign of the coefficient is positive), although the rate of divergence does decline over the four time periods. These results are not in accord with the theoretically expected results of the neoclassical growth model. To be consistent with theoretically expected results the rate of convergence should be increasing and thus the β – coefficient should be negative, statistically significant, and increasing in magnitude across the four time periods.

Table 6.1 Regressions for Per Capita Income Convergence Across MSAs Using Basic Equation

Period	β	R^2 $[\sigma]$
1970-75	.0421	.67
	(.0054)*	[.0064]
1975-80	.0231	.46
	(.0038)	[.0048]
1980-85	.0197	.26
	(.0061)	[.0050]
1985-90	.0013	.01
	(.0121)	[.0211]
1970-90	.0124	.86
	(.0021)	[.0013]

*standard error

Results of Neoclassical Tests of Income Convergence Using Growth Rates

To test whether convergence might be conditional upon other forces affecting metropolitan growth, the Solow-Swan and, more elaborate versions of neoclassical growth theory were tested using equations 4.3 and 4.4, with government expenditures added to the more elaborate version of the model to derive a third fitted form. The dependent variable in the analysis is the growth rate of MSA average per capita income. The variable $\ln Y_0$ is the value of the log of income for the base year. Results are detailed in tables 6.2 through 6.5 for the time periods 1970-75, 1975-80, 1980-85, and in table 6.6 for the entire time span 1970-1990.

Table 6.2 reveals that once the influences of the independent variables are controlled, the sign of the coefficient $\ln Y_0$ becomes negative, as predicted by neoclassical theory. It is, however, not statistically significantly different than zero, indicating that there was neither convergence nor divergence of the growth rate of incomes in the period 1970-75. The growth rates of income did, however, vary positively with growth rates of capital investment and of human capital, of population, level of unionization and so forth.

Table 6.2 Growth Rates 1970-1975

Variable	Basic Solow Swan Model	Elaborate Neoclassical Growth Model	Elaborate Neoclassical Growth Model With Public Investment
Intercept	.047**	.044**	.044**
LnY$_0$	-.0114	-.009	-.0097
Capital Investment	.029***	.026***	.025***
Capital Augmentation		.001	.001
Population	.27***	.26***	.26***
Unionization		.017***	.016***
Tax		.011**	.010**
Human Capital		.041***	.038***
Government Expenditure			.031***
OBS	1,155	1155.00	1155.00
Adj R-squared	.23	.235	.241
F-Value	4.72	4.61	4.59

* 1.66-2.00 **2.01-2.50 ***2.51+

The results for the 1970-75 time period are essentially repeated for the 1975-80, 1980-85, and 1985-90 time periods, with only two exceptions. Coefficients of lnY$_0$ are all negative but not significantly different from zero. All other variables are positively associated with the growth rate of income, except level of unionization, which is significant and positive in 1970-75, 75-80 and 85-90 but significantly negative 1980-85, and the tax variable which turns negative in 1985-90.

Table 6.3 Growth Rates 1975-1980

Variable	Basic Solow Swan Model	Elaborate Neoclassical Growth Model	Elaborate Neoclassical Growth Model With Public Investment
Intercept	.044**	.041*	.041*
LnY_0	-.013	-.012	-.012
Capital Investment	.026***	.022 **	.022**
Capital Augmentation		.001**	.001**
Population	.281***	.276***	.274***
Unionization		.010***	.009***
Tax		.017**	.016**
Human Capital		.031***	.031***
Government Expenditure			.037***
OBS	1155.00	1155.00	1155.00
Adj R-squared	.21	.226	.231
F-Value	4.32	3.97	4.01

*1.65-2.00 **2.01-2.5 ***2.51+

Table 6.4 Growth Rates 1980-1985

Variable	Basic Solow Swan Model	Elaborate Neoclassical Growth Model	Elaborate Neoclassical Growth Model With Public Investment
Intercept	.031**	.030**	.030**
LnY$_0$	-.0007	-.0008	-.0008
Capital Investment	.026***	.022**	.021**
Capital Augmentation		.001**	.001**
Population	.28***	.276***	.274***
Unionization		-.010***	-.009***
Tax		.017***	.016***
Human Capital		.031***	.034***
Government Expenditure			.037***
OBS	1155.00	1155.00	1155.00
Adj R-squared	.247	.251	.257
F-Value	4.28	4.08	4.11

*1.65-2.00 **2.01-2.50 ***2.51+

Table 6.5 Growth Rates 1985-1990

Variable	Basic Solow-Swan Model	Elaborate Neoclassical Growth Model	Elaborate Neoclassical Growth Model With Public Investment
Intercept	.0275**	.0261**	.026**
LnY_0	-.00072	-.00081	-.00084
Capital Investment	.018***	.017**	.016**
Capital Augmentation		.001*	.001*
Population	.275***	.261***	.252***
Unionization		.007**	.007**
Tax		-.010***	-.011**
Human Capital		.019***	.019***
Government Expenditure			.041***
OBS	1155.00	1155.00	1155.00
Adj R-squared	0.24	0.217	0.224
F-Value	3.67	3.81	3.93

*1.65-2.00 **2.01-2.50 ***2.51+

Table 6.6 repeats the three neoclassical analyses for the entire 1970-1990 time span. The sign shifts of the unionization and tax variables are gone, and all hypothesized sources of growth are positively associated with the growth rate of metropolitan income. Surprisingly, the coefficient lnY_0 shifts from negative to positive, but again is not significantly different from zero, so there is no case to be made for the neoclassical hypothesis of conditional convergence.

Table 6.6 Growth Rates 1970-1990

Variable	Basic Solow Swan Model	Elaborate Neoclassical Growth Model	Elaborate Neoclassical Growth Model With Public Investment
Intercept	.031**	.030**	.030**
LnY_0	.00095	.00098	.001
Capital Investment	.020 **	.017**	.013** ,
Capital Augmentation		.001*	.001*
Population	.063***	.061***	.061***
Unionization		.012**	.009**
Tax		.009***	.007***
Human Capital		.021***	.019***
Government Expenditure			.041***
OBS	4620.00	4620.00	4620.00
Adj R-squared	.231	.24	.24
F-Value	6.12	6.22	6.17

*1.65-2.00 **2.01-2.50 ***2.51+

Results of Endogenous Growth Models

Will different specifications of the growth model reveal evidence of divergence or convergence? The results of the different endogenous growth formulations, detailed below, were obtained via estimation of the models described in equations 4.5 and 4.6. Tables 6.7-6.10 provide he results for the time periods 1970-1975, 1975-1980, 1980-1985, 1985-1990 and table6.11 for the entire time span 1970-1990.

For none of the equations in any of the time periods is the coefficient $\ln Y_0$ significantly different from zero, confirming the results presented earlier, although in all time periods except the first, the sign is positive, as suggested by endogenous growth theory. All the hypothesized sources of growth are significant, save for the capital augmentation variable. Growth rates of metropolitan area income do vary systematically, but they appear to be independent of initial levels of income Y_0. In both the endogenous growth and elaborate neoclassical growth formulation there is the behavior of both time and MSA dummies. The effects of both these sets of dichotomous variables are significant. The time dummy effects appear to a large extent to reflect the macroeconomic events and vagaries of the 1970-1990 period. Similarly, the results of the dummy variables show that in fact, the MSA dummies have a considerable effect. The fact is clear-time and place matter in regard to economic growth. Noteworthy, (Table 7.1) is that the year dummy variables follow national macroeconomic phenomenon. That is to say that the standard errors of the year dummies initially increase, peak and show decline. The same is true of the MSA dummies. It should be noted that results of unit root and cointegration tests in Appendix C reveal a tendency toward non-stationarity, but because the time span covers only 21 years these results are controvertible.

Table 6.7 Growth Rates 1970-1975

Variable	Basic Endogenous Growth Model	Regional Growth Theory Augmented Endogenous Growth Model	Regional Growth Theory Augmented Endogenous Growth Model with Government Expenditures
Intercept	0.05**	0.05**	0.05**
LnY_0	-.0034	-.0037	-.0039
Capital Investment	.026**	0.021**	0.019**
Capital Augmentation	.001*	.001	.001
Service		.019**	.016**
Population	0.261***	0.26***	.254***
Human Capital	.049***	0.041***	0.037***
Manufacturing		.051***	.0465***
Government Expenditure			.0912***
Technology	.024***	.023***	.023***
OBS	1155.00	1155.00	1155.00
Adj R-squared	.279	.291	0.311
F-Value	5.89	6.13	6.24

*1.65-2.00 **2.01-2.50 ***2.51+

Table 6.8 Growth Rates 1975-1980

Variable	Basic Endogenous Growth Model	Regional Growth Theory Augmented Endogenous Growth Model	Regional Growth Theory Augmented Endogenous Growth Model with Government Expenditures
Intercept	.041**	.040**	.040 **
LnY_0	.0023	.0031	.0034
Capital Investment	.019*	.018*	0.02
Capital* Augmentation	---	----	----
Population	.21***	.19***	.18***
Human Capital	.041***	.037**	.036**
Service		.04**	.04**
Manufacturing		.031**	.030**
Government Expenditure			.14**
Technology	.026***	.025***	.024***
OBS	1155.00	1155.00	1155.00
Adj R-squared	.297	.314	.336
F-Value	6.23	6.37	6.41

*1.65-2.00 **2.01-2.50 ***2.51+

Table 6.9 Growth Rates 1980-1985

Variable	Basic Endogenous Growth Model	Regional Growth Theory Augmented Endogenous Growth Model	Regional Growth Theory Augmented Endogenous Growth Model with Government Expenditures
Intercept	.036**	.034**	.034**
LnY_0	.0018	.0026	.0029
Capital Investment	0.01	0.01	0.01
Capital Augmentation	---	----	----
Population	.25**	.23**	.22**
Human Capital	.035**	.031**	.031**
Service		.06**	.06**
Manufactures		.04**	.037**
Government Expenditure			.16***
Technology	.031**	.031**	.030**
OBS	1155.00	1155.00	1155.00
Adj R-squared	.291	.314	.327
F-Value	6.11	6.39	6.41

*1.65-2.00 **2.01-2.50 ***2.51+

Table 6.10 Growth Rates 1985-1990

Variable	Basic Endogenous Growth Model	Regional Growth Theory Augmented Endogenous Growth Model	Regional Growth Theory Augmented Endogenous Growth Model with Government Expenditures
Intercept	0.031*	.029 **	.029**
LnY_0	.002	.0027	.0029
Capital Investment	.004*	.001	.001
Capital Augmentation	.001	.001	.001
Population	.27***	.26***	.26***
Human Capital	.029**	.028**	.028**
Service		.03**	.03**
Manufactures		.021**	.019**
Government Expenditure			.19***
Technology	.029**	.028**	.028**
OBS	1155.00	1155.00	1155.00
Adj R-squared	.241	.258	.271
F-Value	5.74	6.11	6.13

*1.65-2.00 **2.01-2.50 ***2.51+

Table 6.11 Growth Rates 1970-1990

Variable	Basic Endogenous Growth Model	Regional Growth Theory Augmented Endogenous Growth Model	Regional Growth Theory Augmented Endogenous Growth Model with Government Expenditures
Intercept	.037**	.037**	.037**
LnY_0	.0019	.0023	.0026
Capital Investment	.015**	.014**	.014**
Capital Augmentation	.001	.001	.001
Population	.24***	.24***	.23***
Human Capital	.032**	.031**	.031**
Service		.05**	.05**
Manufactures		.05***	.05***
Government Expenditure			.11***
Technology	.031**	.030**	.030**
OBS	4620.00	4,620	4,620
Adj R-squared	.281	.312	.321
F-Value	6.03	6.12	6.19

*1.65-2.00 **2.01-2.5 ***2.5+

Results of Tests of σ − Convergence

Tests for the presence of σ − convergence were undertaken as described in equation 4.7. The results in table 6.12 indicate that the dispersion of income has exhibited and modest increase and then remains constant. This is counter to the theoretically expected result which predicts that the log of the dispersion of income will decrease over time. Tests were also undertaken using equation 4.9 to test the effect of the relative shares of manufacturing and service employment on the dispersal of the log of average per capita income. The results are shown in table 6.13. As noted previously, the definition of those employment's which constitute service employment changed in 1980. This leads to a problem of consistency, so thus this analysis is confined to the 1980 through 1990 time period. As is revealed in table 6.13, the log of dispersion is higher than that in table 6.12.

Table 6.12 Period Log of Dispersion

1970-1975	.21
1975-1980	.24
1980-1985	.26
1985-1990	.25
1970-1990	.257

Table 6.13 Period Log of Dispersion

1980-1985	.28
1985-1990	.26
1980-1990	.271

7 Conclusions

Summary and Conclusions

It is now appropriate to draw together the principal conclusions of the empirical work reported in chapter 6. Hypothesis one stated that "The growth rate of income decreases as income increases. The level of absolute β − convergence decreases over time when controlling for initial levels of income." Instead, we have found absolute β -divergence, the magnitude of which declined from 1970-75 until it was statistically insignificant from zero in 1985-90. Hypothesis 2 stated that "The coefficient on the initial level of MSA per capita income (conditional β − convergence coefficient) shows a negative sign when tested using the growth rate of the independent variables." We do indeed find a negative sign for each of the four time periods analyzed, but the coefficient on initial level of income is not significantly different from zero, with or without the augmentation by government expenditures as proposed in hypothesis 2a.

Hypothesis 3 stated that "The coefficient on the initial level of MSA per capita income (conditional β − convergence coefficient) will show a positive sign when tested using endogenous growth variables." We do find a positive sign, but again the associated coefficients on initial income level are not significantly different than zero.

With respect to σ − convergence, hypotheses 4 and 5 state that "The standard deviation of the log of per capita income declines over time" and "The standard deviation of the log of per capita income declines as a function of employment sector composition". We find no clear pattern. Without controlling for sector, dispersion increases rather that decreases, but with the sectoral controls the dispersion while greater decreases.

What is to be made of this? First the growth rate of metropolitan incomes neither converges nor diverges. While a number of factors produce differences in the growth rates of metropolitan incomes, the rate is independent of the initial growth rate.

The factors that influence the growth rates of real per capita metropolitan incomes are: population, government expenditures, human capital, sector composition, tax and unionization rates. What this analysis shows is that when these influences are taken into account, no relationship to initial level of income remains.

With respect to the question of convergence, there is another possibility. The models could have been estimated using OLS without fixed effects, and all of the variance not accounted for by the independent variables would have been lumped into a single error term. Instead, the choice was made to use a fixed effects format, which strips from the error term intercept shifters for each metropolitan area and time period save for the first. Could estimation of these fixed effects have extracted from the model evidence concerning convergence? To explore this possibility, the standard errors of the time coefficients were computed and are presented in table 7.1. Likewise, the dispersion of the dummy variable coefficients for the metropolitan areas was computed again for each model and is presented in table 7.2. For each model, the standard errors of the time variables show a consistent pattern, increasing from 1970-75 to 1980-85, and decreasing thereafter.

Table 7.1 Standard Errors of Time Variables for Neoclassical Models

Period	Basic Classical Model	Augmented Neoclassical Model	Augmented Neoclassical Model with Government Expenditures
1970-75	.009	.008	.008
1975-80	.011	.012	.012
1980-85	.015	.014	.014
1985-90	.013	.012	.012
1970-90	.012	.012	.012

Table 7.2 Standard Errors of Time Variables for Endogenous Models

Period	Basic Endogenous Model	Augmented Endogenous Model	Augmented Endogenous Model with Government Expenditures
1970-75	.009	.008	.008
1975-80	.012	.012	.012
1980-85	.015	.013	.013
1985-90	.012	.011	.010
1970-90	.011	.011	.010

This is the same linkage of inequality to long-term macro-economic rhythms that was noted by Berry, Harpham and Elliot (1995); inequality rises on a long wave, peaks in periods of stagflation and technological transformation that span a long-wave peak and subsequently declines.

A similar rise and fall characterizes the dispersion of the metropolitan-area dummy coefficients (Table 7.2), suggesting that the convergence noted by other investigators might have been an artifact of the time period studied. Instead what is suggested here is a pattern of responsiveness to long term macroeconomic rhythms.

Once this responsiveness is stripped away from the error term by use of a fixed effects format, the residual standard error coefficients for each model and each period are depicted in table 7.3. As can be seen, the standard errors of the model do not vary greatly. In fact, while there is variation between the different formulations, there is little variation over the different time frames.

Table 7.3 Standard Errors of MSA Variables for Classical Models

Period	Basic Classical Model	Augmented Neoclassical Model	Augmented Neoclassical Model with Government Expenditures
1970-75	.017	.016	.016
1975-80	.023	.022	.022
1980-85	.027	.025	.025
1985-90	.024	.024	.024
1970-90	.021	.020	.020

Table 7.4 Standard Errors of MSA Variables for Endogenous Models

Period	Basic Endogenous Model	Augmented Endogenous Model	Augmented Endogenous Model with Government Expenditures
1970-75	.016	.015	.015
1975-80	.021	.020	.020
1980-85	.024	.023	.023
1985-90	.023	.022	.022
1970-90	.020	.019	.019

Table 7.5 Classical Model Residual Standard Error Coefficients

Period	Basic Endogenous Model	Augmented Endogenous Model	Augmented Neoclassical Model with Government Expenditures
1970-75	21.33	19.48	19.27
1975-80	22.87	20.11	19.65
1980-85	23.65	20.95	20.21
1985-90	22.91	19.21	21.02
1970-90	23.08	20.11	20.91

Table 7.6 Endogenous Model Residual Standard Error Coefficients

Period	Basic Endogenous Model	Augmented Endogenous Model	Augmented Endogenous Model with Government Expenditures
1970-75	18.21	18.12	18.17
1975-80	19.31	18.21	18.07
1980-85	19.43	19.29	18.68
1985-90	18.71	19.03	18.74
1970-90	19.06	19.64	18.48

Policy Implications

If the alternative convergence/divergence hypothesis fail, the other components of the contending bodies of growth theory do not. The independent variables play strong and significant roles, with theoretically and intuitively consistent signs. As a consequence, there are clear policy implications.

Most metropolitan statistical areas in the United States have an economic development function at the municipal and/or metropolitan area. These efforts are also common at the state and federal level. Economic development planning efforts are typically geared toward increasing or fostering local economic and employment growth.

In efforts to attract employment-generating firms, jurisdictions have been known to pursue a number of policies such as tax abatements and infrastructure grants to serve as emoluments to lure prospective employers. Similarly, such efforts to retain or to enhance employment-generating activities have been pursued as well.

These efforts are complemented by a host of federal and state programs and policies seeking to enhance the economic prospects for a particularly blighted city, a state or nation as a whole, through a range of policies all seeking to create "a more favorable business climate" or to increase worker productivity, international competitiveness, or whatever other chimera is viewed as a palliative to the particular social and economic ills that are of concern at a particular time. The effects of the variables tested in the several models used in this study shed some light on the determinants of metropolitan growth and thus on the efficiency of those policy initiatives.

First and importantly, history is not destiny: initial level of income has little, if any, effect on subsequent income growth rates.

What about capital investment? The proxy used was investment in new manufacturing equipment. This variable is central to much of neoclassical growth theory and to the worlds of politics and economic development. The variable was not very significant in the various formulations in affecting growth rates, however. A direct policy implication of this finding is that schemes such as investment tax credits for capital goods, or localized abatements intended to stimulate manufacturing employment, are targeted at a variable which has very little effect on income growth rates.

The results for the capital augmentation variable are likewise counterintuitive. The results indicate that the presence of a research university does very little, if anything, to influence either the level or growth rate of metropolitan income. This direct conclusion begs the issue of the desirability of state and local authorities subsidizing research universities to capture direct benefits. A likely role of research universities is to produce outputs and generate externalities which are not limited to the metropolitan area in which they are located; i.e., the spillover effects from the research university benefit the nation or globe as a whole. As a tool for local economic development or income growth, the presence of a research university does not seem to be the way to go for the time period examined.

Population was by far the most significant variable contributing to both levels and growth rates of income. For every time period and for every formulation, population had a large and statistically significant effect on income growth rates and levels. Beside encouraging population growth, the policy implications are unclear. Population is likely to be a strong proxy for agglomeration economies. Cities with more diverse economies tend to be more dynamic and grow faster (Jacobs, 1969; Glaeser, 1990). A precondition for a diverse economy is size. The larger a city the more niches it can support both internally and in the surrounding area which it serves. This suggests that a permissive attitude to continued population growth is appropriate; i.e. that aggressive attempts to impose growth controls will have adverse welfare effects. Thus, policy makers must be fairly circumspect and not rush toward approaches that seek to control growth, however aggressive "the greens" may be.

The rate of unionization was shown to have a small (occasionally negative) yet statistically significant effect on income levels and growth rates. The variation in the rates and the sign of the unionization variable is likely influenced by a host of factors affecting organized labor in the United States, particularly the large segment of organized labor in the manufacturing sector. Beyond this, little can be said about this variable.

The service and manufacturing sectoral variables proved to have varying effects over the time frame of this study. In particular, it appears that changes in the percentage of the work force employed in manufacturing had a significant effect on per capita income growth, especially early in the time frame. This indicates that the presence of manufacturing employment had a significant effect during the early 1970's and its importance has waned with time. The significance of service sector employment is less clear especially if the changes in the composition of this sector are considered. While there are some limitations in the data, the clear indication is that there has been a change in the employment composition of the economy as a whole and MSAs possessing the ascendant sector tend to do better.

The government expenditure variable, while sometimes small, was nonetheless significant throughout the different model specifications and over different time periods. This is important for a number of reasons. First, we see that government expenditures do in fact contribute to growth in per capita income and to per capita income levels. Policy changes can indeed influence metropolitan income growth. The government expenditures variable used on this study measured only total federal expenditures, however. A plausible conclusion to be drawn is that if metropolitan income growth can be influenced by government expenditures it can become an explicit objective of national state macroeconomic policies.

Those variables adjustable by local authorities (capital augmentation, tax rates), appear to have less of an effect on metropolitan income growth than federal expenditures. The fact that incomes among U.S. MSAs are not converging, potentially generates long term public policy challenges. Even with relative factor mobility, a fair number of workers and capital are likely to remain fixed in low growth areas, and local area policies seem inadequate to the task of producing income convergence. Counter to much contemporary thinking, the results point to national rather than local solutions if greater metropolitan equality is to be achieved.

Possible Areas of Further Research

A clear research problem remains. We still do not know whether a neoclassical or an endogenous growth formulation is to be preferred for metropolitan area analysis. We do know that the competing divergence and convergence hypothesis both fail with respect to U.S. metropolitan income growth for the time period 1970-1990. To the extent that divergence and convergence occurred, it appeared to be in lockstep with long-term macroeconomic movements unrelated to the specific determinants of metropolitan growth. The implication of the findings is that a "third way", must be explored if the behavior of metropolitan incomes is to be fully comprehended.

First, the received neoclassical and endogenous growth theories were formulated with national growth and income in mind. A characteristic of nation states is boundaries that restrict factor mobility. The dependence of income growth on initial income levels postulated by both bodies of theory may be an outcome of factor immobility. U.S metropolitan areas are part of an open economy with few restrictions on mobility of the factors of production. Flows of capital, labor, innovation and enterprise take place freely, linking metropolitan areas into a system of interdependent units of observation. Future research must recognize and tackle this problem of spatial interdependence.

Second, macroeconomic influences can sweep though the system with little lag or inhibition, with variation in metropolitan growth appearing as random normal deviates that stretch and contract modestly according to macroeconomic conditions. Future attempts to model metropolitan income growth must be set squarely within the dynamics of a macroeconomic model capable of capturing the longer-term macroeconomic rhythms that stretch and contract income inequality.

Any model that is developed will include the independent variables shown to be significant in this study. Where the models were weakest was in the treatment of technology. To the neoclassical theorists, technology is of course, exogenous, and can be treated as an intercept shifter that "just happens". The endogenous growth theorists believe that technology should be an integral part of any growth model, a view with obvious appeal. The problem is that technology is not just capital goods, it

is ideas and innovations, and some areas have a greater propensity to innovate than others, while other areas are linked by diffusion processes that unfold over space and through time. Only if these processes become part of the third way that is required will metropolitan income growth analysis advance beyond its present state.

Appendix A
List of MSAs Used
in Analysis for 1970-1990

Table A.1 MSA List

MSA Id Number	MSA Name	MSA Id Number	MSA Name
40	Abilene, TX	4520	Louisville, KY-TN
120	Albany, GA	4600	Lubbock, TX
160	Albany-Schenectedy-Troy, NY	4640	Lynchburg, VA
200	Albuquerque, NM	4680	Macon-Warner Robbins, GA
220	Alexandria, LA	4720	Madison, WI
240	Allentown-Bethlehem, PA-NJ	4763	Manchester-Nashua, NH
280	Altoona, PA	4800	Mansfield, OH
320	Amarillo, TX	4880	McAllen-Edinburg-Mission, TX
380	Anchorage, AK	4900	Melbourne-Titusville-Palm Bay, FL
400	Anderson, IN	4920	Memphis, TN-AR-MS
450	Anniston, AL	4992	Miami-Fort Lauderdale, FL
460	Appleton-Oshkosh, WI	5040	Midland, TX

480	Asheville,SC	5082	Milwaukee-Racine, WI
520	Atlanta, GA	5120	Minneapolis-St. Paul, MN-WI
560	Atlantic City, NJ	5160	Mobile, Al
600	Augusta, GA-SC	5170	Modesto, CA
640	Austin, TX	5200	Monroe, LA
680	Bakersfield, CA	5240	Montgomery, AL
720	Baltimore, MD	5280	Muncie, IN
760	Baton Rouge, LA	5320	Muskegon, MI
780	Battle Creek, MI	5360	Nashville, TN
840	Beaumont-Port Arthur, TX	5403	New Bedford-Fall River-Attelboro, MA
880	Billings, MT	5483	New Haven Waterbury-Meriden, CT
920	Biloxi-Gulfport, MS	5523	New London-Norwich, CT
960	Binghampton, NY	5560	New Orleans, LA
1000	Birmingham, AL	5602	New York-Northern New Jersey-Long Island, NY-NJ-CT
1020	Bloomington, IN	5720	Norfolk-Virginia Beach-New Port News, VA
1040	Bloomington-Normal, IN	5800	Odessa, TX
1080	Boise City, ID	5880	Oklahoma City, OK
1123	Boston-Lawrence, MA	5920	Omaha, NE-IA
1140	Bradenton, FL	5960	Orlando, FL
1240	Brownsville-Harlingen, TX	5990	Owensboro, KY
1260	Bryan-College Station, TX	6015	Panama City, FL

1282	Buffalo-Niagra Falls, NY	6020	Parkersburg-Marietta, WV-OH
1300	Burlington, NC	6025	Pascagoula, MS
1320	Canton, OH	6080	Pensacola, FL
1360	Cedar Rapids, IA	6120	Peoria, IL
1400	Champaign-Urbana, IL	6162	Philadelphia-Wilmington-Trenton, PA-NJ-DE-MD
1440	Charleston, SC	6200	Phoenix, AZ
1480	Charleston, WV	6240	Pine Bluff, AR
1520	Charlotte-Gastonia-Roch Hill, NC-SC	6282	Pittsburgh-Beaver Valley, PA
1560	Chattanooga, TN	6323	Pittsfield, MA
1602	Chicago-Gary-Lake County, Il-In-WI	6403	Portland, ME
1642	Cincinnati-Hamilton, OH-KY-IN	6442	Portland-Vancouver, OR-WA
1660	Clarkesville-Hopkinsville, TN-KY	6460	Poughkeepsie, NY
1692	Cleveland-Akron-Lorain, OH	6483	Providence-Pawtucket-Woonsocket, RI
1720	Colorado Springs, CO	6520	Provo-Orem, UT
1760	Columbia, SC	6560	Pueblo, CO
1800	Columbus, GA-AL	6640	Raleigh-Durham, NC
1840	Columbus, OH	6660	Rapid City, SD
1880	Corpus Christi, TX	6680	Reading, PA
1922	Dallas-Fort Worth, TX	6720	Reno, NV
1960	Davenport-Rock Island, IA-IL	6740	Richland-Kennewick-Pasco, WA
2000	Dayton-Springfield, IL	6760	Richmond-Petersburg VA

2020	Daytona Beach, FL	6800	Roanoke, VA
2040	Decatur, IL	6820	Rochester, MN
2082	Denver-Boulder, CO	6840	Rochester, NY
2120	Des Moines, IA	6880	Rockford, IL
2162	Detroit-Ann Arbor, MI	6920	Sacramento, CA
2200	Dubuque, IA	6960	Saginaw-Bay City-Midland, MI
2240	Duluth, MN-WI	6980	St. Cloud, MN
2290	Eau Claire, WI	7000	St. Joseph, MO
2320	El Paso, TX	7040	St. Louis, MO
2360	Erie, PA	7080	Salem, OR
2400	Eugene-Springfield, OR	7120	Salinas-Seaside-Monterey
2440	Evansville, IN-KY	7160	Salt Lake City-Ogden UT
2520	Fargo-Moorehead, ND-MN	7200	San Angelo, TX
2560	Fayetteville, NC	7240	San Antonio, TX
2580	Fayetteville-Springdale, AR	7320	San Diego, CA
2640	Flint, MI	7362	San Francisco, CA
2650	Florence, AL	7480	Santa Barbara-Santa Maria-Lompoc, CA
2670	Fort Collins-Loveland, CO	7510	Sarasota, FL
2700	Fort Meyers-Cape Coral, FL	7520	Savanah, GA
2720	Fort Smith, AR-OK	7602	Seattle-Tacoma, WA
2760	Fort Wayne, IN	7640	Sherman-Denison, TX

2840	Fresno, CA	7680	Shreveport, LA
2880	Gadsen, AL	7720	Sioux City, IA-NE
2900	Gainesville, FL	7760	Sioux Falls, SD
2985	Grand Forks, ND	7800	South Bend-Mishawaka, IN
3000	Grand Rapids, MI	7840	Spokane, WA
3040	Great Falls, MT	7880	Springfield, IL
3060	Greely, CO	7920	Springfield, MO
3080	Green Bay, WI	8003	Springfield, MA
3120	Greensboro/Winston Salem, NC	8080	Steubenville-Weirton, OH-WV
3160	Greenville-Spartanburg, NC	8120	Stockton, CA
3240	Harrisburg-Lebanon-Carlisle, PA	8160	Syracuse, NY
3283	Harford-New Britain-Middletown-Briston, CT	8240	Tallahassee, FL
3320	Honolulu, HI	8280	Tampa-St. Petersburg, FL
3362	Houston-Galveston-Brazoria, TX	8320	Terre-Haute, IN
3400	Huntington-Ashland, WV-KY-OH	8360	Texarkana, TX-AR
3440	Huntsville, AL	8400	Toledo, OH
3480	Indianapolis, IN	8440	Topeka, KS
3520	Jackson, MI	8520	Tucson, AZ
3560	Jackson, MS	8560	Tulsa, OK
3600	Jacksonville, FL	8600	Tuscalosa, AL
3620	Janesville-Beloit, WI	8640	Tyler, TX

3660	Johnson City-Kingsport-Bristol, TN-VA	8680	Utica-Rome, NY
3680	Johnstown, PA	8800	Waco, TX
3720	Kalamazoo, MI	8840	Washington, DC, VA, MD
3740	Kankakee, IL	8920	Waterloo-Cedar Falla, IA
3760	Kansas City, MO-KS	8960	West Palm Beach-Boca Raton-Delray Beach, FL
3810	Killeen-Temple, TX	9000	Wheeling, WV-OH
3840	Knoxville,TN	9040	Wichita, KS
3850	Kokomo, IL	9080	Wichita Falls, TX
3870	La Crosse, WI	9140	Williamsport, PA
3880	Lafayette, LA	9200	Wilmington, NC
3920	Lafayette-West Lafayette, IN	9243	Worcester-Fitchburg-Leomister, MA
3960	Lake Charles, LA	9260	Yakima, WA
3980	Lakeland-Winter Haven, FL	9280	York, PA
4000	Lancaster, PA	9320	Youngstown-Warren, OH
4040	Lansing-East Lansing, MI		
4080	Laredo, TX		
4120	Las Vegas, NV		
4150	Lawrence, KS		
4200	Lawton, OK		
4243	Lewiston-Auburn, ME		
4280	Lexington-Fayette, KY		

4320	Lima, OH
4360	Lincoln, NE
4400	Little Rock-North Little Rock, AR
4420	Longview-Marshall, TX
4472	Los Angeles Anahein-Santa Ana, CA

Appendix B
Results of Cross Section Analyses for Neoclassical and Endogenous Models

B.1 Neoclassical Model Cross Section Results

The results for the 1970 cross section are shown in table 1 below. The dependent variable in the analysis is average per capita income. The results are those of a cross section and those there are no time or place effects. In the results presented below it is clear is that the rate of income divergence tended to about 5% per year for all three variations of the Solow Swan model. Yet, as these results merely examine cross sections, results of convergence are limited to reflect only that particular period of time. Again, the sign of the intercept term is opposite that predicted by neoclassical growth theory. Moreover, the intercepts are all statistically significant.

For all cross sections, the intercept indicates income divergence. Capital investment is significant, but most significant is population. It may be the case that population serves to capture a number of phenomenon which contribute to income. In particular, population may serve as a proxy for agglomeration which comes with size and in turn leads to increased growth. Unionization is fairly significant, as would be expected given the relatively large portion of employment in manufacturing which at that time was unionized. Counterintuitive are the values of the tax coefficient for both versions of the elaborate neoclassical model.

Table B.1 Determinants of Growth 1970

Variable	Basic Solow Swan Model	Elaborate Neoclassical Growth Model	Elaborate Neoclassical Growth Model With Public Investment
Intercept	.051**	.049**	.051**
Capital Investment	.031**	.030**	.027**
Capital Augmentation		0.00	
Population	.26***	.26***	.254***
Unionization		.027**	.021**
Tax		.011*	.011*
Human Capital		.046**	.043**
Government Expenditure			.03**
OBS	232.00	232.00	232.00
Adj R-squared	0.27	.281	.292
F-Value	3.21	3.22	3.19

*1.65-2.00 **2.01-2.50 ***2.51+

Table B.2 Determinants of Growth 1980

Variable	Basic Solow Swan Model	Elaborate Neoclassical Growth Model	Elaborate Neoclassical Growth Model With Public Investment
Intercept	0.04*	0.04*	0.04*
Capital Investment	.024**	.021*	.018*
Capital Augmentation		0.00	0.00
Population	.271***	.261***	.257***
Unionization		-.011**	-.010**
Tax		.014**	.013**
Human Capital		.036**	.034**
Government Expenditure			.039***
OBS	232.00	232.00	232.00
Adj R-squared	.263	.272	.280
F-Value	3.41	3.34	3.22

*1.65-2.00 **2.01-2.50 ***2.51+

Table B.3 Determinants of Growth 1990

Variable	Basic Solow Swan Model	Elaborate Neoclassical Growth Model	Elaborate Neoclassical Growth Model With Public Investment
Intercept	.026**	.025**	.025**
Capital Investment	.017**	.016*	.013*
Capital Augmentation		.000	0.00
Population	.267***	.264***	.262***
Unionization		.004*	.004*
Tax		.011*	.009*
Human Capital		.021**	.019**
Government Expenditure			.042***
OBS	232.00	232.00	232.00
Adj R-squared	0.24	.251	.262
F-Value	3.04	3.11	3.05

*1.65-2.00 **2.01-2.50 ***2.51+

Table B.4 Neoclassical Model Employing Levels

Variable	Basic Solow Swan Model	Elaborate Neoclassical Growth Model	Elaborate Neoclassical Growth Model With Public Investment
Intercept	.036**	.035**	.035**
$\ln Y_0$	.007	.008	0.01
Capital Investment	.022 **	.019**	.013**
Capital Augmentation		.001*	.001*
Population	.277***	.271***	.271***
Unionization		.014**	.012**
Tax		.010***	.0092***
Human Capital		.023***	.021***
Government Expenditure			.044***
OBS	4620.00	4620.00	4620.00
Adj R-squared	.26	.277	0.27
F-Value	6.71	6.81	6.88

*1.65-2.00 **2.01-2.50 ***2.51+

Given that it is widely assumed in neoclassical based research that taxes contribute to economic contraction and job loss and a host of other economic bad's, the positive sign and statistical significance of this coefficient is surprising. Consistent with theory is the value and significance of the human capital coefficient. The value for government expenditure is also counter to results of prior research which found that government expenditures had a marginal result on income. Here, government expenditure exhibits a modest but significant effect.

For the 1980 (Table B.2) cross section what is striking is the decline in the rate of divergence relative to the 1970 (Table B.1) cross section. Also the increase of the effect of population, tax, and government expenditure are not consistent with what is expected. The decrease in the effect of human capital relative to 1970 is unusual. This may result from an increase in the number of college graduates. While human capital is important, the presence of a research university has no effect. This is unusual in that while the output of the university--an individual with a certain level of human capital has an effect on income, the presence of a research university does not. This is particularly vexing since research universities are not confined to producing graduates but also produce research which should produce knowledge, techniques and other results which should contribute to augmenting area income. In comparing the cross sectional results presented above, there are some interesting changes in the values of the determinants of per capita income for the values of the single year cross section for 1980 when compared against those of the single year cross section for 1970. Particularly striking is the change in the value of the UNION coefficient from being significantly positive to significantly negative with respect to its effect on per capita income. This result clearly indicates that change has in fact taken place within the U.S. economy. This is particularly telling when taken together with the fact that the coefficient for MANUF, remains strongly significant in 1980. So while manufacturing employment still has a positive effect on income, unionization does not. This may well be attributable to the shifting of manufacturing jobs from higher wage higher unionized states to lower wage low unionization states. The shift of the manufacturing jobs to these lower wage regions will in turn have an effect to push incomes upward.

In comparing the three cross sections presented above, obvious is the change by 1990 in the magnitude of the determinants and the decline in the rate of income divergence for each successive year. There is a large increase in the effect of government spending and a continued drop in the effect of human capital. As can be seen in the results of the cross sectional analysis for the single year 1990 (Table B.3), there again can be seen very significant changes in the determinants of per capita MSA income, when compared to the values of the coefficients of the exogenous growth variables for the analysis for the years 1970 and 1990. Particularly striking is the decline in the strength and significance of human capital in the 1990 year. This may likely be due to the dramatic increase in the number of college graduates in the 1980s decade. Also noteworthy is an increase in the magnitude and significance of the government expenditures variable. This again, is counter to results yielded by researchers employing a neoclassical formulation to examine determinants of MSA income growth.

As can be seen in table B.4 significantly different results are obtained employing growth rates and levels. Again as in the case of the neoclassical formulation, the use of levels results in higher rates of divergence and greater statistical significance. This is a very significant finding since a large portion of empirical research cited in this work employ the use of levels in their analysis of income growth rates and convergence. The rates of convergence in a number of empirical studies are likely to be overstated.

B.2 Endogenous Model Cross Section Results

In table B.5, results are shown for a cross section for 1970. This analysis used the levels for the year 1970 and not growth rates as in the multi-year analysis results presented below. This and the other single period cross sectional analysis were undertaken and presented to demonstrate the changing character of the determinants of metropolitan area income. In table B.5 below, the intercept term is positive and is both statistically significant and consistent with what is indicated by endogenous growth theory. POP (populations) shows a significant relationship with income. Implicit in this is the role which population and its concomitant efficiencies brought on by agglomeration effects imparts on a regions income. HUMCAP (human capital) also show a positive and significant effect on income. This finding is significant with the assumptions in endogenous growth theory that human capital embodies significant knowledge spillover effects. The results for 1980 exhibit a slightly different pattern.

Table B.5 Determinants of Growth 1970

Variable	Basic Endogenous Growth Model	Regional Growth Theory Augmented Endogenous Growth Model	Regional Growth Theory Augmented Endogenous Growth Model with Government Expenditures
Intercept	.052**	.051**	.051**
Capital Investment	.026**	.022**	.020**
Capital* Augmentation	.002**	.002*	.001*
Population	.231***	.22***	.22***
Human Capital	.052***	.051***	.05**
Service		.030***	.028***
Manufacturing		.08***	.076***
Government Expenditure			.12**
Technology**	.032**	.031**	.030**
OBS	232.00	232.00	232.00
Adj R-squared	.261	.310	0.32
F-Value	3.01	3.48	3.58

*1.65-2.00 **2.01-2.50 ***2.51+

Table B.6 Determinants of Growth 1980

Variable	Basic Endogenous Growth Model	Regional Growth Theory Augmented Endogenous Growth Model	Regional Growth Theory Augmented Endogenous Growth Model with Government Expenditures
Intercept	.046*	.043*	.043*
Capital Investment	.022**	.021**	.021**
Capital Augmentation	.002**	.002**	.001**
Population	.25***	.23***	.23***
Human Capital	.047***	.044***	.041***
Service		.05**	.04**
Manufacturing		.04**	.36**
Government Expenditure			.15***
Technology	.031***	.030***	.029***
OBS	232.00	232.00	232.00
Adj R-squared	.248	.317	.327
F-Value	2.79	3.07	3.12

*1.65-2.00 **2.01-2.50 ***2.51+

In the 1980 cross section, a sharp decrease in the rate of income divergence is evident. Also, a decrease in the importance of human capital is seen. What remains significant although exhibiting some decline is the role of the manufacturing and service sectors. Remaining highly significant is population. The role of research universities as some form of knowledge spillover generator appears not at all. Similarly, the role of the technology variable selected is not as large as expected, plus as indicated above, this variable is highly collinear with population and introduces multicollinearity throughout the different time periods and specifications.

This variable was not included in the results presented, but its coefficient value is presented for purposes of illustration. Clearly, a better proxy for technology is required. For the 19990 cross section presented in table B.7 below, a declining rate of divergence is readily apparent. Also significant is the continued decline in the importance of human capital. Both the role of the service sector and manufacturing continue to be significant.

Table B.7 Determinants of Growth 1990

Variable	Basic Endogenous Growth Model	Regional Growth Theory Augmented Endogenous Growth Model	Regional Growth Theory Augmented Endogenous Growth Model with Government Expenditures
Intercept	.036**	.034**	.033**
Capital Investment	.018**	.016**	.016**
Capital Augmentation	.002**	.002**	.001**
Population	.27***	.25***	.25***
Human Capital	.033***	.032***	.031***
Service		.06**	.05**
Manufacturing		.02***	.02**
Government Expenditure			.19***
Technology	.024**	.0235**	.0225**
OBS	232.00	232.00	232.00
Adj R-squared	.241	.263	.294
F-Value	3.21	3.43	3.51

*1.65-2.00 **2.01-2.50 ***2.51+

Table B.8 Endogenous Growth Model Using Levels 1970-1990

Variable	Basic Endogenous Growth Model	Regional Growth Theory Augmented Endogenous Growth Model	Regional Growth Theory Augmented Endogenous Growth Model with Government Expenditures
Intercept	.041**	.040**	.040**
$\ln Y_0$	.0027	.0032	.0034
Capital Investment	.017**	.016**	.016**
Capital Augmentation	.001	.001	.001
Population	.26***	.26***	.25***
Human Capital	.034**	.034**	.033**
Service		.06**	.06**
Manufacturing		.06***	.058***
Government Expenditure			.16***
Technology	.033**	.032**	.032**
OBS	4620.00	4,620	4,620
Adj R-squared	.301	.327	.337
F-Value	6.12	6.31	6.386

*1.65-2.00 **2.01-2.50 ***2.51+

Appendix C
Unit Root Tests

The Augmented Dickey Fuller (ADF) test is used to test for unit roots and thus examine the stationarity of a time series. This tests the regression of the first difference of the time series against first lagged series, lagged difference terms and a constant time trend. The test is conducted in two ways, only the intercept term is included in the regression, and the inclusion of a linear trend with an intercept. If the coefficient differs significantly from zero then the hypothesis that y contains a unit root is rejected and proves that y is stationary. As can be seen in the results, there is greater amount of non-stationarity when levels are used versus the case for growth rates.

Table C.1 Unit Root Tests for Growth Rates of Average Per Capita Income

MSA	Intercept	Lag	Trend	Lag	MSA	Intercept	Lag	Trend	Lag
40	Fail	2.00	Reject (0.05)	2.00	4520	Reject (0.01)	1.00	Reject (0.01)	0.00
120	Reject (0.01)	0.00	Reject (0.01)	0.00	4600	Reject (0.01)	2.00	Reject (0.01)	2.00
160	Reject (0.01)	2.00	Reject (0.01)	2.00	4640	Reject (0.01)	0.00	Reject (0.01)	0.00
200	Reject (0.01)	0.00	Reject (0.01)	0.00	4680	Reject (0.01)	0.00	Reject (0.01)	0
220	Reject (0.01)	0.00	Reject (0.01)	0.00	4720	Fail	3.00	Reject (0.01)	2.00
240	Reject (0.05)	2.00	Reject (0.01)	2.00	4763	Reject (0.01)	0.00	Reject (0.01)	0
280	Reject (0.01)	0	Reject (0.01)	0	4800	Reject (0.01)	0	Reject (0.01)	0
320	Reject (0.01)	1	Reject (0.01)	0	4880	Reject (0.01)	0	Reject (0.01)	0
380	Reject (0.01)	0	Reject (0.01)	0	4900	Reject (0.01)	0	Reject (0.01)	0
400	Reject (0.01)	1.00	Reject (0.01)	1.00	4920	Fail	2.00	Fail	2.00
450	Reject (0.01)	0.00	Reject (0.01)	0.00	4992	Reject (0.01)	0	Reject (0.01)	0.00
460	Reject (0.01)	0.00	Reject (0.05)	0.00	5040	Reject (0.01)	2.00	Reject (0.01)	2.00
480	Reject (0.01)	0.00	Reject (0.01)	0.00	5082	Reject (0.05)	0.00	Reject (0.01)	0.00
520	Reject (0.05)	2.00	Reject (0.05)	2.00	5120	Fail	4.00	Reject (0.01)	3.00
560	Reject (0.01)	0.00	Reject (0.01)	0.00	5160	Reject (0.01)	0.00	Reject (0.01)	0.00
600	Reject (0.01)	5.00	Reject (0.01)	4.00	5170	Reject (0.01)	0.00	Reject (0.01)	0.00
640	Reject (0.01)	2.00	Reject (0.01)	2.00	5200	Reject (0.01)	0.00	Reject (0.01)	0.00
680	Reject (0.01)	0	Reject (0.01)	0	5240	Reject (0.01)	0	Reject (0.01)	0
720	Reject (0.01)	0.00	Reject (0.01)	0.00	5280	Reject (0.01)	0.00	Reject (0.01)	0.00

760	Fail	3.00	Reject (0.05)	2.00	5320	Reject (0.01)	0.00	Reject (0.01)	0.00
780	Reject (0.05)	0.00	Reject (0.01)	0.00	5360	Reject (0.01)	1.00	Reject (0.01)	0.00
840	Reject (0.01)	0.00	Reject (0.01)	0.00	5403	Rejec (0.01)	0.00	Reject (0.01)	0.00
880	Reject (0.05)	2.00	Reject (0.01)	0.00	5483	Reject (0.01)	0.00	Reject (0.01)	0.00
920	Reject (0.01)	1.00	Reject (0.01)	0.00	5523	Reject (0.01)	3.00	Reject (0.01)	2.00
960	Reject (0.01)	2.00	Reject (0.01)	2.00	5560	Fail	2.00	Fail	1.00
1000	Regect (0.01)	0.00	Reject (0.01)	0.00	5602	Reject (0.01)	0.00	Reject (0.01)	0.00
1020	Reject (0.01)	0.00	Reject (0.01)	0	5720	Reject (0.05)	4.00	Reject (0.01)	3.00
1040	Fail	3.00	Reject (0.01)	2.00	5800	Reject (0.05)	2.00	Reject (0.01)	1.00
1080	Reject (0.01)	0.00	Reject (0.01)	0	5880	Reject (0.01)	0.00	Reject (0.01)	0.00
1123	Reject (0.01)	0	Reject (0.01)	0	5920	Reject (0.01)	0.00	Reject (0.01)	0.00
1140	Reject (0.01)	0	Reject (0.01)	0	5960	Reject (0.01)	1.00	Reject (0.01)	0.00
1240	Reject (0.01)	0	Reject (0.01)	0	5990	Reject (0.01)	0.00	Reject (0.01)	0
1260	Fail	2.00	Fail	2.00	6015	Reject (0.01)	0.00	Reject (0.01)	0.00
1282	Reject (0.01)	0	Reject (0.01)	0.00	6020	Reject (0.01)	5.00	Reject (0.01)	3.00
1300	Reject (0.01)	2.00	Reject (0.01)	2.00	6025	Reject (0.01)	1.00	Reject (0.01)	0.00
1320	Reject (0.05)	0.00	Reject (0.01)	0.00	6080	Reject (0.01)	2.00	Reject (0.01)	1.00
1360	Fail	4.00	Reject (0.01)	3.00	6120	Reject (0.05)	4.00	Reject (0.01)	0.00
1400	Reject (0.01)	0.00	Reject (0.01)	0.00	6162	Reject (0.01)	0.00	Reject (0.05)	0.00
1440	Reject (0.01)	0.00	Reject (0.01)	0.00	6200	Reject (0.01)	0.00	Reject (0.01)	0.00
1480	Reject (0.01)	0.00	Reject (0.01)	0.00	6240	Reject (0.05)	2.00	Reject (0.05)	2.00

1520	Reject (0.01)	0	Reject (0.01)	0	6282	Reject (0.01)	0.00	Reject (0.01)	0.00
1560	Reject (0.01)	0.00	Reject (0.01)	0.00	6323	Reject (0.01)	5.00	Reject (0.01)	4.00
1602	Reject (0.01)	0.00	Reject (0.01)	0.00	6403	Reject (0.01)	2.00	Reject (0.01)	2.00
1642	Reject (0.01)	1.00	Reject (0.01)	0.00	6442	Reject (0.01)	0	Reject (0.01)	0
1660	Reject (0.01)	0.00	Reject (0.01)	0.00	6460	Reject (0.01)	0.00	Reject (0.01)	0.00
1692	Reject (0.01)	0.00	Reject (0.01)	0.00	6483	Fail	3.00	Reject (0.05)	2.00
1720	Fail	3.00	Reject (0.05)	2.00	6520	Reject (0.05)	0.00	Reject (0.01)	0.00
1760	Reject (0.05)	0.00	Reject (0.01)	0.00	6560	Reject (0.01)	0.00	Reject (0.01)	0.00
1800	Reject (0.01)	0.00	Reject (0.01)	0.00	6640	Reject (0.05)	2.00	Reject (0.01)	0.00
1840	Reject (0.05)	2.00	Reject (0.01)	0.00	6660	Reject (0.01)	0.00	Reject (0.01)	0.00
1880	Reject (0.01)	1.00	Reject (0.01)	0.00	6680	Reject (0.01)	0.00	Reject (0.01)	0.00
1922	Reject (0.01)	2.00	Reject (0.01)	2.00	6720	Reject (0.01)	2.00	Reject (0.01)	2.00
1960	Regect (0.01)	0.00	Reject (0.01)	0.00	6740	Reject (0.01)	0.00	Reject (0.01)	0.00
2000	Reject (0.01)	0.00	Reject (0.01)	0	6760	Reject (0.01)	0.00	Reject (0.01)	0.00
2020	Fail	3.00	Reject (0.01)	2.00	6800	Reject (0.05)	2.00	Reject (0.01)	2.00
2040	Reject (0.01)	0.00	Reject (0.01)	0	6820	Reject (0.01)	0	Reject (0.01)	0
2082	Reject (0.01)	0	Reject (0.01)	0	6840	Reject (0.01)	1	Reject (0.01)	0
2120	Reject (0.01)	0	Reject (0.01)	0	6880	Reject (0.01)	0	Reject (0.01)	0
2162	Reject (0.01)	0	Reject (0.01)	0	6920	Reject (0.01)	1.00	Reject (0.01)	1.00
2200	Fail	2.00	Fail	2.00	6960	Reject (0.01)	0.00	Reject (0.01)	0.00
2240	Reject (0.01)	0	Reject (0.01)	0.00	6980	Reject (0.01)	0.00	Reject (0.05)	0.00

2290	Reject (0.01)	2.00	Reject (0.01)	2.00	7000	Reject (0.01)	0.00	Reject (0.01)	0.00
2320	Reject (0.05)	0.00	Reject (0.01)	0.00	7040	Reject (0.05)	2.00	Reject (0.05)	2.00
2360	Fail	4.00	Reject (0.01)	3.00	7080	Reject (0.01)	0.00	Reject (0.01)	0.00
2400	Reject (0.01)	0.00	Reject (0.01)	0.00	7120	Reject (0.01)	5.00	Reject (0.01)	4.00
2440	Reject (0.01)	0.00	Reject (0.01)	0.00	7160	Reject (0.01)	2.00	Reject (0.01)	2.00
2520	Reject (0.01)	0.00	Reject (0.01)	0.00	7200	Reject (0.01)	0	Reject (0.01)	0
2560	Reject (0.01)	0	Reject (0.01)	0	7240	Reject (0.01)	0.00	Reject (0.01)	0.00
2580	Reject (0.01)	0.00	Reject (0.01)	0.00	7320	Fail	3.00	Reject (0.05)	2.00
2640	Reject (0.01)	0.00	Reject (0.01)	0.00	7362	Reject (0.05)	0.00	Reject (0.01)	0.00
2650	Reject (0.01)	1.00	Reject (0.01)	0.00	7480	Reject (0.01)	0.00	Reject (0.01)	0.00
2670	Reject (0.01)	0.00	Reject (0.01)	0.00	7510	Reject (0.05)	2.00	Reject (0.01)	0.00
2700	Reject (0.01)	0.00	Reject (0.01)	0.00	7520	Reject (0.01)	1.00	Reject (0.01)	1.00
2720	Reject (0.01)	0.00	Reject (0.01)	0.00	7602	Reject (0.01)	0.00	Reject (0.01)	0.00
2760	Reject (0.01)	5.00	Reject (0.01)	3.00	7640	Reject (0.01)	0.00	Reject (0.05)	0.00
2840	Reject (0.01)	1.00	Reject (0.01)	0.00	7680	Reject (0.01)	0.00	Reject (0.01)	0.00
2880	Reject (0.01)	2.00	Reject (0.01)	2.00	7720	Reject (0.05)	2.00	Reject (0.05)	2.00
2900	Reject (0.05)	4.00	Reject (0.01)	3.00	7760	Reject (0.01)	0.00	Reject (0.01)	0.00
2985	Reject (0.01)	0.00	Reject (0.05)	0.00	7800	Reject (0.01)	5.00	Reject (0.01)	4.00
3000	Reject (0.01)	0.00	Reject (0.01)	0.00	7840	Reject (0.01)	2.00	Reject (0.01)	2.00
3040	Reject (0.05)	2.00	Reject (0.05)	1.00	7880	Reject (0.01)	0	Reject (0.01)	0
3060	Reject (0.01)	0.00	Reject (0.01)	0.00	7920	Reject (0.01)	0.00	Reject (0.01)	0.00

3080	Reject (0.01)	5.00	Reject (0.01)	3.00	8003	Fail	3.00	Reject (0.05)	2.00
3120	Reject (0.01)	2.00	Reject (0.01)	1.00	8080	Reject (0.05)	0.00	Reject (0.01)	0.00
3160	Reject (0.01)	0	Reject (0.01)	0.00	8120	Reject (0.01)	0.00	Reject (0.01)	0.00
3240	Reject (0.01)	0.00	Reject (0.01)	0.00	8160	Reject (0.05)	2.00	Reject (0.01)	0.00
3283	Fail	3.00	Reject (0.05)	2.00	8240	Reject (0.05)	3.00	Reject (0.01)	2.00
3320	Reject (0.01)	0.00	Reject (0.01)	0.00	8280	Reject (0.01)	0.00	Reject (0.01)	0.00
3362	Fail	3.00	Reject (0.05)	2.00	8320	Reject (0.01)	0.00	Reject (0.01)	0.00
3400	Reject (0.05)	0.00	Reject (0.01)	0.00	8360	Reject (0.01)	0.00	Reject (0.01)	0.00
3440	Reject (0.01)	0.00	Reject (0.01)	0.00	8400	Reject (0.01)	2.00	Reject (0.01)	0.00
3480	Reject (0.05)	2.00	Reject (0.01)	0.00	8440	Reject (0.01)	0.00	Reject (0.01)	0.00
3520	Reject (0.01)	1.00	Reject (0.01)	0.00	8520	Reject (0.01)	0.00	Reject (0.01)	0.00
3560	Reject (0.01)	2.00	Reject (0.01)	2.00	8560	Reject (0.01)	0.00	Reject (0.01)	0.00
3600	Reject (0.01)	0.00	Reject (0.01)	0.00	8600	Reject (0.01)	2.00	Reject (0.01)`	2.00
3620	Reject (0.01)	0.00	Reject (0.01)	0	8640	Reject (0.05)	2.00	Reject (0.05)	1.00
3660	Fail	3.00	Reject (0.01)	2.00	8680	Reject (0.01)	0.00	Reject (0.01)	0.00
3680	Reject (0.01)	0.00	Reject (0.01)	0	8800	Reject (0.01)	0.00	Reject (0.01)	0.00
3720	Reject (0.01)	0	Reject (0.01)	0	8840	Reject (0.05)	1.00	Reject (0.01)	0.00
3740	Reject (0.01)	0	Reject (0.01)	0	8920	Reject (0.01)	1.00	Reject (0.01)	1
3760	Reject (0.01)	0	Reject (0.01)	0	8960	Reject (0.01)	1.00	Reject (0.01)	1.00
3810	Fail	2.00	Fail	2.00	9000	Reject (0.01)	0.00	Reject (0.01)	0.00
3840	Reject (0.01)	0	Reject (0.01)	0.00	9040	Reject (0.01)	0.00	Reject (0.01)	0.00

3850	Reject (0.01)	2.00	Reject (0.01)	2.00	9080	Reject (0.01)	0.00	Reject (0.01)	0.00
3870	Reject (0.05)	0.00	Reject (0.01)	0.00	9140	Reject (0.01)	0.00	Reject (0.01)	0.00
3880	Reject (0.01)	0.00	Reject (0.01)	0.00	9200	Reject (0.01)	0.00	Reject (0.01)	0.00
3920	Reject (0.05)	2.00	Reject (0.01)	1.00	9243	Reject (0.01)	0.00	Reject (0.01)	0.00
3960	Reject (0.01)	0.00	Reject (0.01)	0.00	9260	Reject (0.01)	0.00	Reject (0.01)	0.00
3980	Reject (0.01)	2.00	Reject (0.01)	2.00	9280	Reject (0.01)	0.00	Reject (0.01)	0.00
4000	Reject (0.01)	0.00	Reject (0.01)	0.00	9320	Reject (0.01)	0.00	Reject (0.01)	0.00
4040	Reject (0.05)	3.00	Reject (0.01)	2.00					
4080	Reject (0.01)	0.00	Reject (0.01)	0.00					
4120	Reject (0.01)	0.00	Reject (0.01)	0.00					
4150	Reject (0.01)	0.00	Reject (0.01)	0.00					
4200	Reject (0.01)	2.00	Reject (0.01)	0.00					
4243	Reject (0.01)	0.00	Reject (0.01)	0.00					
4280	Reject (0.01)	0.00	Reject (0.01)	0.00					
4320	Reject (0.01)	0.00	Reject (0.01)	0.00					
4360	Reject (0.01)	2.00	Reject (0.01)	2.00					
4400	Reject (0.05)	2.00	Reject (0.05)	1.00					
4420	Reject (0.01)	0.00	Reject (0.01)	0.00					
4472	Reject (0.01)	0.00	Reject (0.01)	0.00					

Table C.2 Unit Root Tests for Levels of Per Capita Average Income

MSA	Intercept	Lag	Trend	Lag	MSA	Intercept	Lag	Trend	Lag
40	Fail	2.00	Fail	2.00	4520	Reject (0.01)	1.00	Reject (0.01)	0.00
120	Reject (0.01)	0.00	Reject (0.01)	0.00	4600	Reject (0.01)	2.00	Reject (0.01)	2.00
160	Reject (0.01)	2.00	Reject (0.01)	2.00	4640	Reject (0.01)	0.00	Reject (0.01)	0.00
200	Fail	2.00	Fail	1.00	4680	Fail	0.00	Fail	0
220	Fail	0.00	Fail	0.00	4720	Fail	2.00	Fail	1.00
240	Reject (0.05)	0.00	Reject (0.01)	0.00	4763	Reject (0.01)	0.00	Reject (0.01)	0
280	Reject (0.01)	1	Reject (0.01)	1	4800	Reject (0.01)	0	Reject (0.01)	0
320	Fail	2	Fail	1	4880	Reject (0.01)	1	Reject (0.01)	0
380	Reject (0.01)	0	Reject (0.01)	0	4900	Reject (0.01)	0	Reject (0.01)	0
400	Reject (0.01)	0.00	Reject (0.01)	0.00	4920	Fail	1.00	Fail	1.00
450	Fail	5.00	Fail	3.00	4992	Reject (0.01)	1	Reject (0.01)	0.00
460	Reject (0.01)	0.00	Reject (0.05)	0.00	5040	Reject (0.01)	2.00	Reject (0.01)	2.00
480	Reject (0.01)	0.00	Reject (0.01)	0.00	5082	Fail	5.00	Fail	3.00
520	Reject (0.05)	0.00	Reject (0.05)	0.00	5120	Fail	4.00	Reject (0.01)	3.00
560	Reject (0.01)	0.00	Reject (0.01)	0.00	5160	Reject (0.01)	0.00	Reject (0.01)	0.00
600	Reject (0.01)	5.00	Reject (0.01)	4.00	5170	Reject (0.01)	0.00	Reject (0.01)	0.00
640	Fail	2.00	Fail	1.00	5200	Reject (0.01)	0.00	Reject (0.01)	0.00
680	Reject (0.01)	1	Reject (0.01)	0	5240	Reject (0.01)	0	Reject (0.01)	0
720	Reject (0.01)	0.00	Reject (0.01)	0.00	5280	Reject (0.01)	0.00	Reject (0.01)	0.00

760	Fail	2.00	Reject (0.05)	2.00	5320	Reject (0.01)	0.00	Reject (0.01)	0.00
780	Reject (0.05)	0.00	Reject (0.01)	0.00	5360	Reject (0.01)	1.00	Reject (0.01)	0.00
840	Fail	0.00	Fail	0.00	5403	Rejec (0.01)	0.00	Reject (0.01)	0.00
880	Reject (0.05)	2.00	Reject (0.01)	0.00	5483	Reject (0.05)	0.00	Reject (0.01)	0.00
920	Reject (0.01)	1.00	Reject (0.01)	0.00	5523	Reject (0.01)	3.00	Reject (0.01)	2.00
960	Reject (0.01)	2.00	Reject (0.01)	2.00	5560	Fail	2.00	Fail	1.00
1000	Reject (0.05)	0.00	Reject (0.01)	0.00	5602	Reject (0.01)	0.00	Reject (0.01)	0.00
1020	Reject (0.01)	0.00	Reject (0.01)	0	5720	Reject (0.05)	4.00	Reject (0.01)	3.00
1040	Fail	3.00	Reject (0.01)	2.00	5800	Reject (0.05)	2.00	Reject (0.01)	1.00
1080	Reject (0.01)	0.00	Reject (0.01)	0	5880	Fail	0.00	Fail	0.00
1123	Fail	2	Fail	0	5920	Reject (0.01)	4.00	Reject (0.01)	2.00
1140	Reject (0.01)	0	Reject (0.01)	0	5960	Reject (0.01)	1.00	Reject (0.01)	0.00
1240	Reject (0.01)	0	Reject (0.01)	0	5990	Reject (0.01)	1.00	Reject (0.01)	1
1260	Fail	2.00	Fail	2.00	6015	Reject (0.01)	0.00	Reject (0.01)	0.00
1282	Reject (0.01)	1	Reject (0.01)	0.00	6020	Reject (0.01)	5.00	Reject (0.01)	3.00
1300	Fail	1.00	Fail	1.00	6025	Reject (0.01)	1.00	Reject (0.01)	0.00
1320	Reject (0.05)	0.00	Reject (0.01)	0.00	6080	Reject (0.01)	2.00	Reject (0.01)	1.00
1360	Fail	2.00	Fail	1.00	6120	Fail	3.00	Fail	2.00
1400	Reject (0.01)	0.00	Reject (0.01)	0.00	6162	Reject (0.01)	0.00	Reject (0.05)	0.00
1440	Reject (0.01)	1.00	Reject (0.01)	0.00	6200	Reject (0.01)	0.00	Reject (0.01)	0.00
1480	Reject (0.01)	0.00	Reject (0.01)	0.00	6240	Reject (0.05)	2.00	Reject (0.05)	2.00

1520	Reject (0.01)	0	Reject (0.01)	0	6282	Fail	2.00	Fail	1.00
1560	Reject (0.01)	0.00	Reject (0.01)	0.00	6323	Reject (0.01)	5.00	Reject (0.01)	4.00
1602	Reject (0.01)	0.00	Reject (0.01)	0.00	6403	Reject (0.01)	2.00	Reject (0.01)	2.00
1642	Reject (0.01)	1.00	Reject (0.01)	0.00	6442	Reject (0.01)	0	Reject (0.01)	0
1660	Reject (0.01)	0.00	Reject (0.01)	0.00	6460	Reject (0.01)	0.00	Reject (0.01)	0.00
1692	Reject (0.01)	0.00	Reject (0.01)	0.00	6483	Fail	3.00	Fail	1.00
1720	Fail	2.00	Fail	1.00	6520	Reject (0.05)	0.00	Reject (0.01)	0.00
1760	Reject (0.05)	0.00	Reject (0.01)	0.00	6560	Fail	0.00	Fail	0.00
1800	Reject (0.01)	0.00	Reject (0.01)	0.00	6640	Reject (0.05)	2.00	Reject (0.01)	0.00
1840	Reject (0.05)	0.00	Reject (0.01)	0.00	6660	Reject (0.01)	0.00	Reject (0.01)	0.00
1880	Reject (0.01)	1.00	Reject (0.01)	0.00	6680	Reject (0.01)	0.00	Reject (0.01)	0.00
1922	Reject (0.01)	2.00	Reject (0.01)	2.00	6720	Reject (0.01)	2.00	Reject (0.01)	2.00
1960	Fail	1.00	Fail	1.00	6740	Reject (0.01)	0.00	Reject (0.01)	0.00
2000	Reject (0.01)	0.00	Reject (0.01)	0	6760	Fail	0.00	Fail	0.00
2020	Fail	2.00	Fail	2.00	6800	Reject (0.05)	2.00	Reject (0.01)	2.00
2040	Fail	0.00	Fail	0	6820	Reject (0.01)	1	Reject (0.01)	0
2082	Reject (0.01)	0	Reject (0.01)	0	6840	Reject (0.01)	1	Reject (0.01)	0
2120	Reject (0.01)	0	Reject (0.01)	0	6880	Reject (0.01)	0	Reject (0.01)	0
2162	Reject (0.01)	0	Reject (0.01)	0	6920	Reject (0.01)	1.00	Reject (0.01)	1.00
2200	Fail	2.00	Fail	1.00	6960	Reject (0.01)	0.00	Reject (0.01)	0.00
2240	Reject (0.01)	0	Reject (0.01)	0.00	6980	Reject (0.01)	0.00	Reject (0.05)	0.00

2290	Reject (0.01)	2.00	Reject (0.01)	2.00	7000	Fail	0.00	Fail	0.00
2320	Reject (0.05)	0.00	Reject (0.01)	0.00	7040	Reject (0.05)	2.00	Reject (0.05)	2.00
2360	Fail	2.00	Fail	2.00	7080	Reject (0.01)	0.00	Reject (0.01)	0.00
2400	Reject (0.01)	0.00	Reject (0.01)	0.00	7120	Reject (0.01)	3.00	Reject (0.01)	2.00
2440	Reject (0.01)	0.00	Reject (0.01)	0.00	7160	Reject (0.01)	2.00	Reject (0.01)	2.00
2520	Reject (0.01)	0.00	Reject (0.01)	0.00	7200	Reject (0.01)	1	Reject (0.01)	0
2560	Fail	0	Fail	0.00	7240	Reject (0.01)	0.00	Reject (0.01)	0.00
2580	Reject (0.01)	0.00	Reject (0.01)	0.00	7320	Fail	2.00	Fail	1.00
2640	Reject (0.01)	0.00	Reject (0.01)	0.00	7362	Reject (0.05)	0.00	Reject (0.01)	0.00
2650	Fail	0.00	Fail	0.00	7480	Reject (0.01)	0.00	Reject (0.01)	0.00
2670	Reject (0.01)	1.00	Reject (0.01)	0.00	7510	Reject (0.01	0.00	Reject (0.01)	0.00
2700	Reject (0.01)	0.00	Reject (0.01)	0.00	7520	Reject (0.01)	1.00	Reject (0.01)	1.00
2720	Reject (0.01)	0.00	Reject (0.01)	0.00	7602	Reject (0.01)	0.00	Reject (0.01)	0.00
2760	Reject (0.01)	5.00	Reject (0.01)	3.00	7640	Reject (0.01)	0.00	Reject (0.05)	0.00
2840	Reject (0.01)	1.00	Reject (0.01)	0.00	7680	Reject (0.01)	0.00	Reject (0.01)	0.00
2880	Reject (0.01)	2.00	Reject (0.01)	2.00	7720	Fail	1.00	Fail	1.00
2900	Reject (0.05)	2.00	Reject (0.01)	1.00	7760	Reject (0.01)	0.00	Reject (0.01)	0.00
2985	Reject (0.01)	0.00	Reject (0.05)	0.00	7800	Reject (0.01)	5.00	Reject (0.01)	4.00
3000	Reject (0.01)	1.00	Reject (0.01)	0.00	7840	Reject (0.01)	2.00	Reject (0.01)	2.00
3040	Reject (0.05)	2.00	Reject (0.05)	1.00	7880	Fail	2	Reject (0.01)	0
3060	Reject (0.01)	0.00	Reject (0.01)	0.00	7920	Reject (0.01)	0.00	Reject (0.01)	0.00

3080	Reject (0.01)	5.00	Reject (0.01)	3.00	8003	Fail	3.00	Reject (0.05)	2.00
3120	Reject (0.01)	2.00	Reject (0.01)	1.00	8080	Reject (0.05)	0.00	Reject (0.01)	0.00
3160	Reject (0.01)	0	Reject (0.01)	0.00	8120	Reject (0.01)	0.00	Reject (0.01)	0.00
3240	Reject (0.01)	0.00	Reject (0.01)	0.00	8160	Reject (0.05)	2.00	Reject (0.01)	0.00
3283	Fail	3.00	Reject (0.05)	2.00	8240	Fail	0.00	Fail	0.00
3320	Reject (0.01)	2.00	Reject (0.01)	2.00	8280	Reject (0.01)	0.00	Reject (0.01)	
3362	Fail	1.00	Fail	0.00	8320	Fail	0	Fail	0.00
3400	Reject (0.01)	0.00	Reject (0.01)	0.00	8360	Reject (0.01)	1.00	Reject (0.01)	0.00
3440	Fail	0.00	Fail	0.00	8400	Reject (0.01)	0.00	Reject (0.01)	
3480	Reject (0.01)	0.00	Reject (0.01)	0.00	8440	Fail	0.00	Fail	0.00
3520	Fail	2.00	Fail	1.00	8520	Reject (0.01)	1.00	Reject (0.01)	0.00
3560	Reject (0.01)	3.00	Reject (0.01)	2.00	8560	Reject (0.01)	0.00	Reject (0.01)	
3600	Reject (0.01)	2.00	Reject (0.01)	2.00	8600	Fail	0.00	Fail	0.00
3620	Reject (0.01)	0.00	Reject (0.01)	0.00	8640	Reject (0.01)	5.00	Reject (0.01)	
3660	Fail	2.00	Fail	0.00	8680	Reject (0.01)	1.00	Reject (0.01)	
3680	Reject (0.01)	0.00	Reject (0.01)	0.00	8800	Fail	1.00	Fail	0.00
3720	Reject (0.01)	1.00	Reject (0.01)	0.00	8840	Fail	1.00	Fail	1.00
3740	Reject (0.01)	0.00	Reject (0.01)	0.00	8920	Fail	0.00	Fail	0.00
3760	Fail	2.00	Fail	0.00	8960	Reject (0.01)	1.00	Fail (0.01)	1.00
3810	Reject (0.01)	0.00	Reject (0.01)	0.00	9000	Reject (0.01)	0.00	Reject (0.01)	0.00
3840	Reject (0.01)	0.00	Reject (0.01)	0.00	9040	Reject (0.01)	0.00	Reject (0.01)	0.00

3850	Reject (0.01)	1.00	Reject (0.01)	0.00	9080	Fail	0.00	Fail	0.00
3870	Reject (0.01)	2.00	Reject (0.01)	2.00	9140	Reject (0.01)	0.00	Reject (0.01)	0.00
3880	Reject (0.05)	2.00	Reject (0.05)	1.00	9200	Fail	5.00	Fail	4.00
3920	Fail	1.00	Fail	0.00	9243	Reject (0.01)	0.00	Reject (0.01)	0.00
3960	Reject (0.01)	0.00	Reject (0.01)	0.00	9260	Reject (0.01)	0.00	Reject (0.01)	0.00
3980	Reject (0.01)	2.00	Reject (0.01)	2.00	9280	Reject (0.01)	0.00	Reject (0.01)	0.00
4000	Reject (0.01)	0.00	Reject (0.01)	0.00	9320	Reject (0.01)	0.00	Reject (0.01)	0.00
4040	Reject (0.05)	2.00	Reject (0.01)	2.00					
4080	Reject (0.01)	1.00	Reject (0.01)	0.00					
4120	Reject (0.01)	0.00	Reject (0.01)	0.00					
4150	Fail	0.00	Fail	0.00					
4200	Reject (0.01)	2.00	Reject (0.01)	0.00					
4243	Reject (0.01)	0.00	Reject (0.01)	0.00					
4280	Reject (0.01)	0.00	Reject (0.01)	0.00					
4320	Reject (0.01)	1.00	Reject (0.01)	0.00					
4360	Fail	2.00	Fail	2.00					
4400	Reject (0.05)	1.00	Reject (0.05)	1.00					
4420	Reject (0.01)	1.00	Reject (0.01)	0.00					
4472	Reject (0.01)	0.00	Reject (0.01)	0.00					

Bibliography

Aitcheson, J. *The Statistical Analysis of Compositional Data.* London, Chapman and Hall, Ltd. (1986).

Aschauer, David A. "Is Public Expenditure Productive?" *Journal of Monetary Economics*, March 1989, 23 (2), pp.177-200.

Barro, Robert J., "Economic Growth in a Cross Section of Countries." *Quarterly Journal of Economics* 106 (May 1991): 407-443.

Barro, Robert J., N. Gregory Mankiw, and Xavier Sala-i-Martin. "Capital Mobility in Neoclassical Models of Growth." *American Economic Review* 85 (March 1995): 103-115.

Barro, Robert and Xavier Sala-i-Martin. "Convergence across States and Regions." *Brookings Papers on Economic Activity* (1991): 107-182.

Barro, Robert and Xavier Sala-i-Martin. *Economic Growth.* Boston, MA: McGraw-Hill, Inc. (1995).

Baumol, William J. "Productivity Growth, Convergence, and Welfare: What the Long-Run Data Show." *American Economic Review* 76 (December 1988): 1155-1159.

Baumol, William J. and Edward N. Wolff: "Productivity Growth, Convergence, and Welfare: Reply." *American Economic Review* 78 (December 1988): 1155-1159.

Bernard, Andrew B. and Charles I. Jones. "Technology and Convergence." *The Economic Journal* 106 (July 1996): 1037-1044.

Bernard, Andrew B. and Steven N. Durlauf. "Interpreting Tests of Convergence Hypothesis." *Journal of Econometrics* 71 (Mar/April 1996): 161-173.

Berndt, Ernst R. and Hansson, Bengt. "Measuring the Contribution of Public Infrastructure Capital in Sweden." *Scandinavian Journal of Economics* (Supplement 1992): S151-72.

Berry, Brian J.L., Harpham, Edward J. and Elliot, Euel. "Long Swings in American Inequality: The Kuznets Conjecture Revisited," *Papers in Regional Science: The Journal of the Regional Science Association International* 74, 2: 153-174.

Borts, George H. and Stein, Jerome L. *Economic Growth in a Free Market*, Columbia University Press, New York (1964).

Crihfield, John B. and Panggabean, Martin P.H., "Growth and Convergence in U.S. Cities." *Journal of Urban Economics* 138 (January 1995): 138-165.

Crihfield, John B. and Panggabean, Martin P.H.,"Is public infrastructure productive? A metropolitan perspective using new capital stock estimates" *Regional Science and Urban Economics* 25 (1995) 607-630.

De Long, J. Bradford. "Productivity Growth, Convergence, and Welfare: Comment." *American Economic Review* 78 (December 1988): 1138-1154.

Durlauf, Steven N. "Controversy on the Convergence and Divergence of Growth Rates: An Introduction." *The Economic Journal* 106 (July 1996): 1016-1018.

Galor, Oded. "Convergence? Inference from Theoretical Models." *The Economic Journal* 106 (July 1996): 1956-1096.

Garcia-Mila, Teresa and McGuire, Therese J. "The Contribution of Publicly Provided Inputs to States' Economies." *Regional Science and Urban Economics* 22 (June 1992): 229-42.

Greene, William H. *Econometric Analysis,* 2nd Edition. Prentice Hall, Englewood Cliffs, NJ, 1993.

Haan, Wouter J. Den. "Convergence in Stochastic Growth Models: The Importance of Understanding Why Income Levels Differ." *Journal of Monetary Economics* 35 (1995): 65-82.

Holtz-Eakin, Douglas. "Public Sector Capital and the Productivity Puzzle." *Review of Economics and Statistics*, February 1994, 76 (1), pp. 12-21.

Hulten, Charles R. and Schwab, Robert M. "Regional Productivity Growth in U.S. Manufacturing, 1951-78." *American Economic Review,* March 1984, 74 (1), pp.152-62.

Kim, Yeong Seok. *Reappraisal of the Convergence Hypothesis from the Perspective of Endogenous Growth Theory*, Doctoral Dissertation, The University of Texas at Dallas 1997.

Krugman, Paul. *Development, Geography and Economic Theory.* MIT Press, Boston 1995.

Krugman, Paul. *Trade and Economic Geography* MIT Press, Boston 1991.

Mankiw, N. Gregory, David Romer, and David W. Weil. "A Contribution to the Empiric's of Economic Growth." *Quarterly Journal of Economics* 107 (1992): 402-437.

Munnell, Alicia H. "How Does Public Infrastructure Affect Regional Economic Performance?" *New England Economic Review,* September/October 1990, pp.11-32.

Nadiri, M. Ishaq and Mamuneas, Theosofanis P. "The Effects of Public Infrastructure and R & D Capital on the Cost Structure and Performance of U.S. Manufacturing Industries." *Review of Economics and Statistics* 76 (February 1994): 23-37.

Pack, Howard. "Endogenous Growth Theory: Intellectual Appeal and Empirical Shortcomings." *Journal of Economic Perspectives* 8 (Winter 1994): 55-72.

Perloff, Harvey S., Dunn, Edgar S., Lampard, Eric E., Muth, Richard F,. *Regions, Resources, and Economic Growth.* The Johns Hopkins Press, Baltimore 1960.

Quah, Danny T. "Empirical Cross-section Dynamics in Economic Growth." *European Economic Review* 37 (1993a): 426-434.

Quah, Danny T. "Empirics for Economic Growth and Convergence." *European Economic Review* 40 (1996a): 1353-1375.

Rao, Bhaskara, B. *Cointegration For the Applied Economist.* St. Martins Press, New York, 1994.

Romer, Paul. "Increasing Returns and Long-run Growth." *Journal of Political Economy* 94 (October 1986): 1002-1037.

Romer Paul."Endogenous Technological Change." *Journal of Political Economy* 98 (October 1990a):71-102.

_____."Human Capital and Growth: Theory and Evidence." *Carnegie-Rochester Conference Series on Public Policy* 32 (1990c):251-286.

_____. "Idea Gaps and Object Gaps in Economic Development." *Journal of Monetary Economics* 32 (1993): 543-573.

_____."The Origins of Endogenous Growth." *Journal of Economic Perspectives* 8 (Winter 1994): 3-22.

_____."Why, Indeed, in America? Theory, History, and the Origins of Modern Economic Growth." *AEA Papers and Proceedings* 86 (May 1996): 202-206.

Rostow, W.W. *Theorists of Economic Growth from David Hume to the Present.* Oxford, New York 1990.

Sala-i-Martin, Xavier. "Cross-sectional Regressions and the Empirics of Economic Growth." *European Economic Review* 40 (1996a): 1325-1352.

_____. "Regional Cohesion: Evidence and Theories of Regional Growth and Convergence." *European Economic Review* 40 (1996a): 1325-1352.

_____."The Classical Approach to Convergence Analysis." *The Economic Journal* 106 (July 1996b): 1019-1036.

Sherwood-Call, Carolyn. "The 1980's Divergence in State per Capita Income: What Does it Tell Us?" *Economic Review: Federal Reserve Bank of San Francisco* No 1 (1996): 14-25.

Solow, Robert M. "A Contribution to the Theory of Economic Growth" *Quarterly Journal of Economics* 70 (1956): 65-94.

_____."Perspective on Growth Theory." *Journal of Economic Perspectives* 8 (Winter 1994): 45-54.

Swan, Trevor W. "Economic Growth and Capital Accumulation". *Economic Record* 32 (November 1956): 334-361.

U.S. Bureau of the Census, *Census of Manufacturers,* various.

_____, *Current Population Reports*, various.

_____, *Consolidated Federal Funds Report*, various.

U.S. Bureau of Economic Analysis, *Personal Income by Major Source and Earnings by Major Industry*, 1969-88.

U.S. Bureau of Labor Statistics (BLS), *Employment and Earnings*, May Issues and unpublished.

U.S. National Center for Education Statistics, *Digest of Education Statistics*, annual, various.

Index